PEACE COMES DROPPING SLOW

Maura,

Best wishes

I hope the work

Brian

PEACE COMES DROPPING SLOW

Brian Lennon

Community Dialogue

First published in 2004 by
Community Dialogue
373 Springfield Road
Belfast BT12 7DG
Northern Ireland
Tel: + 44 028 9032 9995
Fax: + 44 028 9033 0482
Email: admin@communitydialogue.org
Website: www.communitydialogue.org

Printed by Perfect Print, Belfast

Dedication

To all who took part in Community Dialogue events between 1997 and 2004, to the staff and members who made these happen, and to our friends and colleagues in Stanford Center for Conflict and Negotiation who helped our thinking about dialogue.

Acknowledgements

Many people have contributed to this book, as it is a reflection on six years' listening to dialogue between divided groups. Some participants attended many events, some only a few. Their sharing was often painful and difficult. Many may find their thoughts reflected in the text.

Others commented directly on the text: Chris O'Halloran, Gerry Ruddy, Gerry O'Hanlon, Cathy Molloy, Dominic Bryan, Bronagh Hinds, Mairead Nic Craith, Frank Sammon, Nigel McCullough and the Community Dialogue staff – David Holloway, Anne Carr, Kay Nellis, Genevieve Lennon, Theresa Cullen and Peadar McKenna. Norma McConville, Dolores Considine and Nan McKinnon gave much time to discussion of some of the ideas. As well, some of these, together with David Gaffney, took on the difficult task of proof reading. Samantha Askin helped with administration.

Byron Bland, Lee Ross, David Holloway, Steve Stedman, Brenna Powell and others from the Stanford Center on Conflict and Negotiation have been incredibly supportive to Community Dialogue over many years. Through many hours of discussion they helped us develop our theory and practice of dialogue. They were also most generous hosts to us during several visits.

The Community Relations Council helped with a publishing grant.

My sincere thanks to all of them.

And I shall have some peace there,
For peace comes dropping slow,
Dropping from the veils of the morning to where the cricket sings;
There midnight's all a glimmer, and noon a purple glow,
And evening full of the linnet's wings.

William Butler Yeats, *The Lake Isle of Innisfree*

Contents

Preface

Everything about the peace process in Northern Ireland is contested: When did it start? Who made the most important contribution? Who were the greatest blockers? What role did violence play? Was there an agreement? Was the process a total fraud? How do we handle the past?

In 1998, a few months before the Belfast Agreement, a group of Unionists, Nationalists, Loyalists, Republicans and others, came together to form Community Dialogue. They disagreed about most subjects, except one: the importance of dialogue among groups divided by the conflict. Between 1998 and 2004 they brought together people from divided communities to hear one another's feelings, values and experiences of the conflict about the 1998 Agreement. The organisation provided a forum where people, especially those from the Community Sector such as womens', local development and community relations groups, could talk and listen to those whom they saw as their enemies. The instinct for this came from a belief that ordinary people were to a large extent excluded from the peace process, especially in its early stages. Perhaps this was inevitable. Nonetheless it was also a source of major problems because deals worked out behind closed doors had to be sold to the wider public.

By 2004 Community Dialogue had run over 500 general events, including half-day and evening seminars, nearly 200 local group meetings, over 50 one or two-night residentials, 19 youth events and almost 100 internal dialogues. In that period there were also over 30 newspaper articles, 24 publications and 24 radio programmes, some of a considerable length. All these were attempts to publicise the perceptions we were hearing and to encourage further dialogue around them. Many of these events were deeply painful for those who took part, but almost all also said they found them challenging and that they led to new understanding. This book is a reflection on what they said.

At the end of Community Dialogue events there was seldom much agreement. During this period we in Northern Ireland were divided about our past, present and future. Nor is the purpose of the book to

win agreement. Rather, as with all Community Dialogue events, it is designed to encourage further dialogue, critical thinking and questioning: to ask people to probe themselves more deeply by asking:
- What is it that you really want?
- Why do you want it?
- What can you live with, given that others want something different?

We hope that people will look at the points with which they disagree and ask why it is that others hold those views. What experiences have led them to that position?

In many of our dialogues people tended to address the current issues of the day. Yet these issues came out of a wider framework and the first part of the book attempts to describe this and to analyse the factors at work in it.

The second chapter, 'A Sulky Stalemate?', takes a snapshot of the situation in 2004 shortly after the 2003 election which was dominated by the DUP and Sinn Féin. At this time the Assembly was suspended because of disagreement over 'guns and government', paramilitaries were still active, Sinn Féin had not joined the Policing Board, segregation had increased, the community remained both politically divided and physically segregated, and there was considerable tension at interface areas. At the same time violence was at a comparatively low level. This section reflects many of the perceptions which came up in our dialogues.

The third chapter, 'From Victimhood to Survival?', looks at the issue which probably was the most dominant in our dialogues: how to handle the past. No matter what topic we proposed participants returned again and again to the past. This was not surprising. Over 3500 were killed in Northern Ireland during the conflict out of a total population of less than 1.5 million people. The web of pain involved in these figures stretched from immediate family and friends through work colleagues to the wider public who felt fear and anger at the killings. Tens of thousands were physically injured. Almost 20,000 were imprisoned. The unavoidable trauma which was and is a legacy of all this was reflected in our dialogues.

The fourth chapter, 'Beyond the Stalemate?', looks at options for the future. Will we continue to operate in Northern Ireland in two highly segregated groups, with no basic agreement about the past, present or future? Will we move towards agreement, while still retaining our separate aspirations? Or will we come up with something different? What impact will the EU and the wider world have on us? What contribution will Northern Ireland make to the EU or to other conflict situations? Again these issues figured often in our dialogues.

The fifth and final chapter looks at Community Dialogue's process and discusses some theoretical issues about this.

The violence in Northern Ireland lasted for more than 35 years. Like all conflicts it was brutal and often seemingly mindless. This book was written ten years after the first IRA cessation on 31 August 1994, followed shortly afterwards by the Loyalist ceasefire of 13 October. At the time these raised enormous hopes. The next 10 years were to show a mixed picture as violence declined considerably but divisions and bitterness remained strong. Yet at the end of the period there seemed a real prospect that the DUP, the strongest critics of the Agreement and Sinn Féin, the political wing of Republicans, might together form a devolved government. Yeats's line, 'Peace comes dropping slow', seems entirely appropriate as a title for a reflection on this process.

Community Dialogue as an organisation takes no party-political position on any issue. This is because we think it better to raise questions than answer them. This is also a useful strategy, because coming as we do from many differing and opposing backgrounds it is unlikely that we would agree on much. The present volume is no exception. It is being published by Community Dialogue in the hope that it may be a stimulus to dialogue. The views in it remain those of the author.

1

Framing the Process

GOVERNMENTS, PARAMILITARIES AND OTHERS

INTRODUCTION

The Northern Ireland peace process was part of a long journey, with many ups and downs. In that respect it has been similar to processes elsewhere in the world where enemies began to find ways other than violence to handle their differences. It was a series of stops and starts, of three steps forward and one step, or sometimes four steps, back. It was a journey of pain, failed hopes, deep longing, insults, sacrifices; of people and groups reaching out to others, victims letting go of the past, others not doing so; of perpetrators admitting their wrong and asking for forgiveness, others justifying what they did, of governments lying and covering up, and also of governments devoting incredible energies to a problem in which there were few votes.

'Peace process' in other words does not refer to a comfortable train journey in a first class carriage through beautiful countryside in great weather, with friends you have cherished all your life. Rather it was sometimes like being stuck in a small boat in the middle of a vicious storm, with people who have hurt you deeply, whom you don't trust a whit, and wishing you could be anywhere else in the world than on that boat with those people. At other times it was an experience of deep richness as one learnt of suffering and the response to it by people caught in incredibly difficult situations.

The central element in the peace process was the 1998 Agreement. The framework of the peace process was important because the Agreement was only one element in a much larger picture. Some elements of the Agreement may fail, but others will continue. Further, many changes which took place involved the interests of the London and Dublin Governments and will remain under their control, and these will continue whether or not people in Northern Ireland like them.

The following were critical elements in the peace process and without each of these it would not have happened:
- The role of the two Governments, and the influence of the European Community on them.
- Military stalemate.
- Leadership among most of the groups involved.
- Time to adjust to new and painful change.
- Ambivalent language.
- Democratic structures and international encouragement.
- Economic change, particularly among UUP supporters.

This chapter now looks at each of these in turn.

THE ROLE OF THE TWO GOVERNMENTS

The recent background to the Northern Ireland peace process started in 1973. In that year both the British and Irish Governments joined the EEC. They did so for their own interests, hoping that the Common Market would give them an opportunity to develop their economies by increasing trade links with other countries and by opening up new markets.

There was also a visionary aspect to the EEC: in 1870, 1914 and 1939 France, Germany and other countries were caught up in terrible wars that left millions dead. The visionaries who set up the EEC in 1952 wanted to build political connections between the countries of Europe so that war could never happen again. The extraordinary thing is that they succeeded to the extent they did. None of the members of the EEC have gone to war with each other since and there exist cooperation, common policies and laws across a broad spectrum of European life.

In this context the Northern Ireland conflict embarrassed the two Governments, it was financially costly and the violence had a negative impact on the relationship between the two countries.

The conflict was not of vital interest to the US, but given the size of the Irish vote it was of some interest to political leaders. Ronald Reagan is said to have raised the issue frequently with Margaret Thatcher. In Bill Clinton's case his involvement clearly went beyond the needs of his country and can only be explained on the basis of personal interest.

Apart from joining the European Community there were other changes which impacted on the British-Irish relationship. Military developments after World War II meant that Northern Ireland was no longer as important to the UK in terms of security. However, some British interests remained unchanged. They remained implacably opposed to any settlement which removed Northern Ireland from the UK against the wishes of its inhabitants. Such an outcome would have undermined the basis of the union between the countries in the UK, and the British Government was never going to consent to this. Because of this the IRA could never have succeeded in its objective of forcing the British Government to accept a United Ireland. Tragically its consistently made the mistake of comparing the British Government's attitude to Northern Ireland to its historical attitude to the colonies: the colonies were not part of the UK, and the British let them go only when there was a majority in favour of this.

The Republic of Ireland, for its part, became more confident as a country through participating as an equal member with the other 11 EU States. It began to revise its view of Northern Ireland. Membership of the EU slowly reduced its economic dependence on the UK. However, the need to address the Northern issue and the gradual changes in Irish nationalism slowly led to a closer relationship with the UK as well. The US connection was also important to the Republic, not least because of the 40 million Americans of Irish descent.

Over the years between 1973 and 1985 and particularly in the final year of this phase, the two Governments agreed on a joint analysis of and approach to the problem and this emerged as the Anglo-Irish Agreement of 1985.

The Anglo-Irish Agreement of 1985
The 1985 Anglo-Irish Agreement was the institutional expression of the new mutual interests of both States in reaching a compromise on the conflict. Under this the two Governments accepted that the conflict was one of a double minority: Nationalists were a minority within Northern Ireland and Unionists a minority in the context of the whole island. Each had different and conflicting aspirations. The right to pursue these aspirations was recognised, but only if done peacefully. The British gave the Irish Government a consultative role about decisions affecting Northern Ireland. Both accepted that if the two communities in Northern Ireland agreed, a devolved power-sharing government should be set up. If the majority of people in Northern Ireland chose a United Ireland that would be facilitated.

Both Governments gained from the Agreement through better relations with each other and approval on the world stage. The critical new element was a reduction in the nationalism with which both approached the issue. This eventually enabled them to stop seeing the problem as an internal issue on the one hand, or one of colonialism on the other, and instead to see it as a problem of a double minority.

The Anglo-Irish Agreement was critical to everything that followed. It meant that neither community within Northern Ireland could use the London or Dublin Government against the other because while the Governments might still disagree, they recognised that what they had in common was greater than their divisions. Before this each Government had tended to act as if one of the groups in Northern Ireland were its own clients. Now that gradually changed. Further, civil servants from both jurisdictions began to meet in the European Community several times a week. This further developed a process which had begun when the two States joined the Community. It helped each understand better the needs of the other and also how their institutions worked.

Positive results of the involvement of the two Governments
The time and resources devoted by both Governments to the peace process over a protracted period was both significant and at times unusual: for example, Tony Blair and Bertie Ahern showed great determination in sticking with the process when often it seemed completely hopeless, in marked contrast to the somewhat haphazard attention given by the Governments to the conflict in previous decades; significant because both were highly skilful negotiators.

The positive impact of the outside Governments on Northern Ireland was in marked contrast to many other conflict situations. For example, in the Middle East there is really only one powerful outside group, the US, and it is strongly biased in favour of the Israelis. The external Arab States, while nominally favouring the Palestinians and while also providing some military support, remained ambivalent and divided in their response. The Cyprus situation had some closer parallels: both Turkey and Greece are external to the island, but both are heavily involved in the conflict. The EU had an even greater role than in Northern Ireland because it has the power to accept or reject Turkey as an EU member (and Greece would have a voice in that decision).

The 1998 Agreement
The negotiations which eventually led to the 1998 Agreement took place in a context in which there were already limits to what any group could achieve. These li Under the 1985 Agreement the British

remained in control of final decisions on controversial issues such as parades. Many of these were against what Unionists wanted. This introduced a new balance of power between Unionists and Nationalists. While Nationalists could not blame the Irish Government for decisions - since the Irish Government had no decision-making power within Northern Ireland - Unionists were faced with the fact that the Government they had seen as their guardians - the British - now sometimes made decisions apparently against their interests. There was nothing Unionists could do against this, as they learnt when over 100,000 protested against the 1985 Agreement but failed to overturn it. This encouraged a sense of betrayal among Unionists and fostered much of the bitterness which followed the Agreement. These limits meant, among other things, that:

- There would never be a settlement which forced the majority of the people of Northern Ireland into a United Ireland.
- There would never be devolved government in Northern Ireland without the consent of the majority of both Unionists and of Nationalists.
- Recognition would have to be given to both British and Irish identities within Northern Ireland.
- There would be a role for the Irish Government, but it would be a consultative one, not one of joint authority.
- What happened in Northern Ireland would be part of wider processes - the needs of the two Governments, their membership of the EU, US-British and US-Irish intergovernmental relationships - and the people of Northern Ireland would have only limited influence over what went on in those processes.

The Agreement had three strands:
- Strand 1: Internal to Northern Ireland, (issues dealing with the Assembly, the Executive, requirements that the consent of both Unionists and Nationalists would be needed to approve disputed motions).
- Strand 2: North-South structures, (bodies dealing with issues such as waterways, tourism, education and transport), with the Northern section accountable to the Assembly and the Southern to the Dáil)
- Strand 3: Irish-UK institutions.

It also contained a series of commitments by the British Government to appoint commissions to review policing (subsequently the Patten

Commission), criminal justice and Human Rights, to give support for the Gaelic and Scots-Irish languages, and a three paragraph passing mention of victims.

Frequently during the peace process people spoke as if the Agreement had failed. This was because internal Northern Ireland structures had collapsed. Yet the wider changes brought about by the Agreement survived. So, for example, the London Government could choose to take the advice of the Dublin Government, or it could do a deal with Republicans about changes in policing, etc. Northern Ireland politicians and people could not block the two Governments when and if they chose to act together on matters within their power. So Strand Two (North-South) and Strand Three (London/Dublin, East-West) continued even when Strand One (Northern Ireland) was suspended.

This was the essential element the two Governments introduced into the conflict in the 1985 Agreement: they changed from opposing each other to working together on the conflict, and there was nothing opponents of this within Northern Ireland could do about it.

Each Government took risks in the peace process. The British Government were in secret talks with Sinn Féin long before the Irish Government knew. This was difficult for them, as can be seen by John Major's comment - while the contacts were in progress - that it would sicken his stomach to talk to the IRA. The Government also persuaded Jim Molyneaux not to reject the whole process at the time of the Downing Street Declaration in 1993. They took the formal decision to suspend the Executive on each occasion before David Trimble resigned. Because they did this they were able to reverse the suspension later without the requirement of a new vote to approve a First Minister, a vote which would have failed because the Unionists would not have supported it.

The Irish Government gave leadership by agreeing to meet the IRA before its cessation of violence - and the IRA was at least as much a threat to the stability of the Republic as it was to Northern Ireland.

MILITARY STALEMATE AND PARAMILITARY LEADERSHIP

A second element which helped the process was the military stalemate. Both the IRA and the British security forces were able to hurt each other, the IRA by attacking the British mainland, the British by planting informers and killing or arresting IRA activists. But neither side could deliver a knock-out blow.

For the IRA to achieve a United Ireland they would have had to impose losses on the security forces heavy enough to persuade the

British Government to expel from the UK one of the four countries which make up the Union, against the will of the majority of that country. That was always highly unlikely. To do so would have destabilised the constitutional basis of the UK as a whole and strengthened the hands of those in Scotland and Wales who wanted independence. No British Prime Minister was going to countenance this seriously.

From 1976 on the British Government started the policy of 'Ulsterisation'. This put the RUC rather than the British army in the front line of the violence, and this led to less British army deaths. The Government also removed special category status from political prisoners, thus in their eyes making them ordinary criminals. This in turn led to the hunger strikes, the outcome of which gave Republicans a sense of what could be gained politically. At the same time British intelligence continued to impact on Republicans, which made it more difficult for the IRA to operate militarily.

From about 1990 the number of loyalist murders matched and eventually exceeded the number of republican murders. Many Loyalists believe that this led ordinary Catholics to put pressure on the IRA for a ceasefire and that this was a major element in persuading the IRA to end the violence. Most Nationalists doubt this. However, the loyalist killings succeeded in something else: they made it more difficult for the IRA to present their struggle as a noble struggle for Irish freedom. Instead it was increasingly seen as a nasty, dirty, tit-for-tat, sectarian blood bath which shamed the island as a whole in the eyes of the world.

There was never majority support within the nationalist community for IRA violence: Sinn Féin only gradually challenged for the leadership of the nationalist community when it became clear that the IRA were moving to end the violence. Republicans could have continued the violence, but it would have been on the basis of maintaining their ideals, not of achieving their goals.

All this increased pressure on Republicans to move towards a peace settlement. For their part the British army recognised they could not defeat the IRA. It was therefore in the interests of both sides to find a way out of a stalemate from which both were suffering.

Yet the violence continued for years after each side was aware of this. That is not unusual in conflicts. During the Cold War both the US and the Soviet Union knew that if they ever used nuclear arms the other side would respond with such force that they themselves would be destroyed. Yet for years each side kept developing these arms even though they knew they could never use them.

One reason for this is that any major change of direction by a movement is often seen as being unfaithful to the past and this forms one of the barriers to resolving political conflicts. Further, conflicts take on a life of their own, often no longer addressing the underlying original causes.

The military stalemate therefore left republican paramilitaries with a choice: did they want to continue with violence which would never achieve their stated aim and leave them isolated politically; or did they want to look for a new way forward?

For their part, the British Government were happy to seek alternatives - within certain limits - provided they were convinced the IRA wanted to change and that this would end the violence, especially on the British mainland.

Republicans and the cessation of violence

The military stalemate impacted more on Republicans than on Loyalists. Loyalists wanted to maintain the status quo. Republicans wanted to change it. The stalemate meant they were not advancing their goals through violence. So some among them began to look for other ways. This was not easy. It meant changing a central belief: that they could defeat British forces in Ireland through violence. Finding an alternative way to persuade them to leave Ireland meant a break with the past. It meant facing accusations of betrayal from other Republicans who continued to reject constitutionalism.

Throughout the 20th century Republicans had split every time there were moves towards constitutional politics. Gerry Adams, Martin McGuinness and others had been central in opposing such moves in the mid-1970s. Yet it was these same people, now leaders in the republican movement, who began to make the first tentative moves towards politics in the 1980s. At the time it was highly unlikely that they could succeed in bringing the movement with them without a major split. Yet, for the most part this is what they achieved: there were dissident Republicans who rejected the ceasefire, but they were a small percentage. That was a major and unlikely achievement of the Adams leadership. Outsiders who only saw continued intelligence gathering, arms procurement, charges of spying, Republicans accused of working with FARC in Columbia and other incidents, missed the point that for many Republicans the major step was to engage in a peace process in which they would cease killing British security forces. The last soldier killed by the IRA was Stephen Restorick in South

Armagh in 1997.

The move towards politics was helped also by the experience of IRA members in prison. Many studied for degrees in politics, sociology, law and other areas and were also involved in on-going debates and political analysis. This helped educate the rank and file about political aims and tactics. Republicans were therefore able to develop a series of political positions, not only on Northern Ireland constitutional politics, but on other conflict situations. Groups set up to lobby on behalf of the prisoners also developed organisational and other political skills and this was crucial in widening Sinn Féin's political base.

The most important single event which helped politicise Republicans was the 1981 hunger strikes. The British Government's attempt to criminalize the IRA was intended to present the conflict as one caused by terrorists attacking the legitimate government, and to downplay issues of nationalism. In fact this policy was doomed to failure because even at the point of arrest and trial, paramilitaries were charged under Special Powers, which meant they were not ordinary prisoners. But it also played on a deeply emotional chord among Republicans. They had always maintained a close link with their prisoners, and they were never going to allow them to be designated as 'criminals'. While the wider nationalist community was ambivalent about this issue a large majority supported the hunger strikers when they began to die. This development was helped by nationalist dislike of Margaret Thatcher.

The death of Bobby Sands and the other hunger strikers had a strong impact on Republicans themselves. In the words of one participant at a Community Dialogue seminar: 'I wanted to burn this place (the North) to the ground when he died'. There was a lot of street violence. Over sixty people died in the summer of 1981. Republicans began to see the potential of political action. This was not obvious in advance. They were divided among themselves as to whether or not they should put Bobby Sands up for election in 1981. Those opposing the move felt there was a high chance he would be defeated, which would mean a set back. However, when the elections went ahead and Republicans won, the rank and file saw the potential benefits of politics.

Electoral politics introduced one other element: Republicans' success at the polls depended on movement towards peace. When they appeared to be going in that direction their votes went up, when they were not their votes went down. Their political support was also influenced by the judgement of Nationalists on British Government policy towards the IRA. When this was seen as harming doves within the Republican movement, or when Nationalists as a whole resented it, Sinn Féin's vote increased.

In the 1985 Agreement the British Government said they were willing to move out of Northern Ireland if the majority of its people asked them to do so. This helped the process whereby Republicans began to accept that their problem lay not only with the British Government, but also with the British people within Northern Ireland, the Unionists. These were not going to go away.

From the secret contacts between the Government and the IRA, the British knew there was an element among Republicans who might be interested in a move towards peace. They did not know what they would demand in turn. Nor did they know if they could bring the rest of the IRA with them. For their part Republicans did not know what response the British would make should there be an end to violence: would they release the prisoners, recognise the mandate of Republicans, set up all-Ireland institutions, or start a process of withdrawal from Northern Ireland?

The decision of John Hume to engage with Republicans was crucial. This eventually led to direct contacts with the Dublin Government. This was an important change. Before this the Dublin Government, particularly under Garret FitzGerald, had been vehemently opposed to contact with Republicans, because, as he saw it, Republicans were at least as big a threat to the Republic as they were to anyone else.

Hume also helped develop contacts between Republicans and the US Government and this in turn led to the perception of a pan-nationalist front. This greatly strengthened the doves among Republicans: political gains began to look no longer like a vague possibility, but as something tangible which could greatly strengthen the movement as a whole.

The pan-nationalist front was a myth in so far as it was sold as something which would lead to a United Ireland. Neither the London nor the Dublin Government was interested in this outcome. Nor was the US. They wanted political stability and an end to violence so that Northern Ireland would no longer be a political problem. Nonetheless the pan-nationalist front helped deal with one of the greatest of republican fears: that they would be isolated politically if they gave up violence. (Ironically their violence was the greatest cause of their political isolation). Ending violence also offered Republicans the chance of 'respectability' and influence.

The pan-nationalist front was a nightmare for Unionists. In part this was because so many of them knew nothing about the mindset of the Dublin Government or the people of the Republic. Had this not been the case they would have known that the Dublin Government was certainly not interested in taking over Northern Ireland with all its problems and costs.

It is not clear what Republicans hoped would emerge from the Talks process. Their ultimate aim was of course a British withdrawal from Northern Ireland based on a single referendum held in the whole of Ireland. They were opposed to the idea of a Northern Ireland Assembly or Executive on the grounds that this would strengthen Northern Ireland as a political entity. They wanted the RUC to be replaced with a new police force and the withdrawal of the British army. They also wanted their prisoners released, human rights legislation and support for the Irish language.

In the event they won early release of prisoners, more resources for the Irish language, a review of the criminal justice system, commissions on Human Rights and policing (the Patten Report), they were accepted into the talks process prior to decommissioning, their electoral success won them two ministries in the Devolved Government, and North-South bodies were set up.

None of these concessions were particularly remarkable. Early release of prisoners, while painful to many, was a small price for the British Government to pay for an end to violence, and there was a precedent in the early release of the 1950s IRA border campaign prisoners. Nor did the Government have any great problem with giving more resources to the Irish language. The review of the criminal justice system, and the commissions on Human Rights and policing were more far reaching because - in the case of the Human Rights Commission - it would have implications for the UK as a whole. But changes in these areas would have been forced on the British Government in any case by EU legislation.

The setting up of North-South bodies also had a precedent in the 1974 Sunningdale settlement - although it was never implemented. With the improved relationship between the two Governments since the Anglo-Irish Agreement of 1985 it was always likely that North-South cooperation would be institutionalised.

Finally, the success of Sinn Féin at the polls could have been available to them at any stage had Republicans not been involved in violence, and had they been more successful at an earlier stage in selling their political programme to the electorate.

Republicans also accepted the following compromises:

- The principle of consent under which there would be no change in the constitutional status of Northern Ireland unless a majority in both North and South voted in separate referenda for a United Ireland. In that case the two Governments would set in motion steps to bring about a United Ireland.
- The setting up of the Assembly and the Executive. (Republicans had to change their Constitution before they could take their places on these).
- The Patten Commission on policing (even though they later found it difficult to accept the recommendations, and had further difficulty when in their view the British Government failed to implement Patten).

The irony was that within two years of their 1997 cessation Republicans who had opposed the setting up of the Assembly were determined to be included in the devolved Government in Stormont.

Military stalemate on its own was not enough to lead to the peace process. It needed the response of Republicans for this to happen, and this in turn needed the leadership of the Adams' wing. This meant taking risks, such as asking the movement to accept the Northern Ireland Assembly and Executive, and the report of the Patten Commission on policing. In part Gerry Adams maintained his position by taking a step forward only when he was sure he had the support of the vast majority of the movement. That was one reason why he carried the coffin of Thomas Begley, an IRA member who killed himself along with nine bystanders when the bomb he was planting in a Shankill Road fish shop exploded prematurely, in October 1993: non-Republicans asked how he could possibly do this if he was interested in peace. The answer was that had he not done so he would have been seen as betraying his own side. Further, he was a Republican and as such he would have wanted to carry the coffin of someone he saw as a comrade-in-arms. This simply illustrates the fact that the peace process was about setting up institutions in which bitterly opposed enemies could find a way eventually to work together.

Republicans were helped change by the prospect of being included in politics in Northern Ireland as equals with everyone else. In their view equality had to come first. With this in place the need for arms would disappear and then there would be an end to violence. The unionist view was exactly the opposite: in order to be accepted into democratic politics Republicans would have to prove their credentials by showing they had given up violence first.

At the time of the 1994 cessation Republicans retained their paramilitary capacity, as they were to show less than two years later in the attack at Canary Wharf in London. So it was they themselves who decided to end their violence. The decision was not imposed on them from the outside. At the same time the the history of the Troubles had shown that they could not achieve their stated objective of a United Ireland through violence.

The loyalist ceasefire
In the mid-1960s Loyalism was controlled by right-wing Protestants. Many claimed they went into paramilitarism because of the influence of people like Ian Paisley. However, during their time in jail some of these abandoned sectarianism and developed political thinking. They were later to play a key role in persuading other Loyalists to abandon violence.

Many Loyalists argued that they wanted to maintain the Union and protect their communities. In their view they existed only because of the IRA. They saw themselves as doing the job that the security forces could not do because they were held back by laws. While the republican movement claimed that their war was against the State, Loyalists saw much of the IRA campaign directed at their own communities. In the loyalist view, then, the IRA waged a sectarian war and their own violence was a response to this.

Many of their targets were innocent Catholics. Some Loyalists viewed this as appropriate because they saw all Catholics as either Republicans or republican supporters and therefore traitors to the State: each Catholic killed was one less threat to the Union. Others thought it was strategic to attack innocent Catholics because it gave the message to the wider nationalist community that they would pay a price for IRA actions. They hoped this would lead to pressure on the IRA from within the Catholic community.

Given their claim that their violence was reactive some argued it was logical that a loyalist ceasefire would come soon after the IRA cessation of 31 August 1994. However, others argued against the ceasefire on the grounds that the IRA were being merely tactical. As with Republicans, so also among Loyalists, leadership was an important ingredient in persuading the different groups to end violence. The loyalist apology which expressed 'abject and true remorse' was an important contribution at the time.

Over the years Loyalists had produced various suggestions for a political way forward, including *Common Sense*, written by John

McMichael in 1987, and also proposals for independence, although these were always going to be dismissed by Nationalists because in their view they gave insufficient protection to minorities. With the IRA cessation, however, Loyalists faced a problem. They had been defending Northern Ireland against the IRA. If the IRA really stopped violence what role could Loyalists have in the future?

Most Nationalists who had been opposed to violence were prepared to forget past Republican violence and support Sinn Féin inclusion in government. Increasing numbers were even prepared to vote for them, considering them effective in championing wider nationalist concerns. Within the unionist community, however, Loyalists had ambivalent support at best. Many would quietly acknowledge that they were needed during the conflict but few were prepared to support them politically when it came to voting and many would have liked them to simply disappear. This may in part have been due to Loyalists' failure to put more effort into its political development. But it was also due in large part to Unionism's ambiguous relationship with Loyalists, viewing them as a necessary evil on the one hand, immoral and illegitimate on the other.

To a degree Loyalists were also the victims of class politics within the unionist community. One of the results of focussing on the unionist-nationalist conflict was that the interests of working-class Protestants were neglected. Further, it was they, not better-off Protestants, who bore the brunt of the conflict, both in killing Nationalists and in suffering casualties themselves. It was only after 1994 that - at least in the public eye - Loyalists began to show an awareness of the way they had been used by others in the Protestant community. The fear of nationalist gains always made it difficult to focus on class issues.

Loyalists were nowhere near as united as Republicans. At the ceasefire they were already split between the UVF and UDA and they fragmented further not only with the LVF splitting from the UVF, but also with internal factions developing within many of the groups.

Finally, the majority of Loyalists suffered from a lower educational achievement than Republicans, many of whom used their time in jail to gain qualifications and degrees. This was largely because at the start of the Troubles more Protestants than Catholics were employed in industries such as ship building in which book learning was not required for many of the jobs. Catholics had never had the same entry to State subsidised jobs and so realised that education was vital to their interests. Economic changes during the Troubles led to a downsizing of the manufacturing sector and a growth of a more knowledge based economy. Because of their improved education working-class Catholics benefited more from this than working-class Protestants. Loyalists were therefore seen to benefit less than Republicans from the peace process and this increased the bitterness of many.

Ambivalent role of paramilitaries
The role of paramilitary leaders has been ambiguous. On the one hand they participated in and led groups which carried out some of the most terrible deeds in the history of this island. On the other hand many played a crucial role in keeping their followers involved in ceasefires, however imperfect, and in renegotiating new ceasefires when existing ones broke down. They did this in a context where they were often scapegoated as being the only cause of violence. It is therefore true that without the contribution of the paramilitaries violence would have been greatly reduced, but also that the reduction of violence which took place during the peace process would not have happened.

The IRA cessation and the loyalist ceasefire of 1994 were critical moments in the peace process. They meant at least that violence would be reduced. They did not mean, as we know to our regret, that it would be over. At the time of the ceasefires many questions remained unanswered:
- Could the cessation and the ceasefire be maintained?
- What role could former paramilitaries play in constitutional politics?
- What would be done about prisoners convicted of crimes arising from the Troubles?
- How could the understanding between the two Governments be developed?
- Could the constitutional parties, the parties linked to paramilitaries, and the two Governments agree not only on the underlying constitutional questions, but also about issues such as power-sharing, the day-to-day running of government, and North-South or East-West bodies?
- What would happen to victims?
- How would we handle the past?

The ceasefires opened the possibility that those formerly engaged in violence could enter the constitutional mainstream. This meant a change from the UUP-SDLP negotiations which had been going on in a stop-start way since 1974: now both Unionists and the SDLP would have to face the real possibility of Sinn Fein being part of any future power sharing arrangement.

THE ROLE OF CONSTITUTIONAL PARTIES AND OTHERS
The Ulster Unionist Party (UUP), like other parties, was a broad church with many different groupings. Its central aim was to defend the Union. It had a strong integrationist wing who wanted to copper-fasten the Union and avoid devolution. Jim Molyneaux, former leader of the UUP, accurately foresaw that the IRA cessation would undermine integration. He said it 'started destabilising the whole population in Northern Ireland. It was not an occasion for celebration, quite the opposite' (*Independent*, 10 July 1999).

For many Unionists their greatest nightmare was to see Republicans in government. At the start of the process it was inconceivable to them that a group who had murdered members of the security forces for over 30 years, who remained unrepentant and who were dedicated to overthrowing the State, could end up in government.

Others, some of whom were opposed to Republicans in government and some who were not, resisted the involvement of the Irish Government in Northern Ireland. This was against the background of UUP opposition to the 1985 Anglo-Irish Agreement. There was a difference, however, in the years immediately before the 1998 Agreement: many Unionists realised their opposition to the 1985 Agreement had been ineffective and that the two Governments could choose to ignore them again. The alternative was to negotiate. Further, these negotiations would have to include the Irish Government.

At the time of the ceasefires Unionists faced a further dilemma. If there was to be an agreement this would involve negotiating with Republicans, albeit indirectly through the two Governments and other intermediaries, with the possibility that this would lead to Republicans being in government, despite the fact that this was what many wanted to avoid. This inevitably led to blocking and delaying tactics. At the same time, if Republicans were serious about moving towards peace, was it better, from a unionist point of view, to have them inside or outside the process? For many years in the process, Unionists now argue, Republicans did not engage effectively in the Talks. Either they were outside the process because of IRA violence, or else, as Unionists saw it, rather than negotiate they merely repeated republican rhetoric. However, towards the beginning of 1998, key

Unionists began to believe that Republicans wanted to engage seriously, because they did not withdraw from the Talks even though their opposition to a Northern Ireland Assembly was proving unsuccessful.

Other Unionists remained opposed to entering government with Sinn Féin. Reasons for this included feelings about what Republicans had done in the past, religious views which opposed political partnership with unrepentant terrorists, and the contradiction of Sinn Féin being linked to a private army while taking part in democratic politics.

During the process Unionists frequently felt marginalised as the British Government focussed on Sinn Féin. In fact once the IRA declared a cessation this was probably inevitable because the primary aim of the British Government was to prevent them returning to violence.

It should have been obvious that any agreement was going to include Sinn Féin, because a central motive for the British Government's involvement was to ensure an end to republican violence and the obvious way to do this was to draw them into government. Yet several Unionists pointed out to us the shock that many negotiators experienced in the week before the 1998 Agreement when George Mitchell produced the first draft of the Agreement precisely because it would give Sinn Féin a seat in government. Up to this negotiations had been about the separate parts of the Agreement. This was the first time that people saw the full picture.

The UUP focussed on decommissioning as a sign that the violence was over. For many it became the Holy Grail. Some later saw this as a mistake and came to accept that Republicans used decommissioning to extract on-going concessions. The wider community found these continuous concessions 'debilitating', in the words of one Unionist.

Arguably many Unionists who voted for the Agreement - estimated at barely over 50% - did so in the expectation that they were getting 'peace'. 'Peace' meant different things to different people but it included the idea that violence was at an end and it did not include continuing enquiries directed against unionist interests, such as actions of the security forces and the renaming of the RUC.

David Trimble is often condemned by Nationalists for not giving leadership. In fact he was always ahead of his own community. Had he not led them into government on four occasions with Sinn Féin, while the IRA was still active, the devolved government would not have been set up. Equally, if he had not collapsed the Executive on four occasions he would not have survived as leader. These decisions were crucial and they enabled the process to survive.

For its part the DUP, led by Ian Paisley, also wanted devolution, but without Sinn Féin. Indeed some only became open to the idea of power-sharing with the SDLP after the 1990-91 talks. Throughout the negotiations they were able to present a harder face than the UUP by highlighting the painful decisions made by Unionists who supported the Agreement: tolerating early release of prisoners (this was a British Government decision), going into government with Sinn Féin, etc. Electorally this helped them as unionist voters progressively distanced themselves from the Agreement. It is estimated that over 100,000 Unionists voted in the Agreement referendum who have not voted since and most of these were probably Yes voters. As a result the proportion of unionist Yes voters dwindled considerably in the years after the referendum. Many Unionists would have found it difficult in any case to share power with Sinn Féin, but a considerable proportion were willing to do so in the context of what they saw as an end to violence. Decommissioning became the litmus test for this, and by the time the IRA eventually destroyed some weapons it was too little too late for many.

Like the UUP, the DUP were determined to maintain as large a security-force presence as possible, to ensure that there were no changes in the RUC which they saw as having been the front line against terrorism, to block early release of prisoners and the emergence of North-South bodies. On all these issues they failed. So Unionists, like Republicans, had to face many painful compromises during the process.

The DUP's role was seen by many as entirely negative. Yet they gave a voice to those who for a variety of reasons opposed the process. Without this more might have turned to violence. They also stood for the principle that no party should be in government while still linked to arms. While individuals in the party can certainly be challenged about their previous links with paramilitaries, the pressure from the DUP was an important element in bringing the IRA to the point where public consideration was given by Gerry Adams in 2004 to their ceasing all activity. At the end of that summer it seemed as if the DUP were about to take a more positive role by entering into serious negotiations with Sinn Féin, albeit doing so through the British Government.

Policy in the SDLP was dominated by John Hume. His decision to engage in negotiations with Sinn Féin was a crucial factor in helping

Republicans edge towards a cessation of violence. In this process he brought with him the influence he had developed over twenty years in Belfast, Dublin, London and Washington.

Many Unionists believe they could have had a power-sharing deal with the SDLP, without Sinn Féin, in the 1991-92 talks had it not been that Hume was engaged in secret talks with Adams and so did not want an agreement which excluded Sinn Féin. Secondly, many in his own party had no idea what he was involved in. This was made all the more difficult for them by threats and hoax bomb attacks against them by Loyalists. At one stage there was pressure on Hume from members of his own party to end the contact with Adams. Thirdly, by bringing Sinn Féin into the political process Hume inevitably made electoral life more difficult for his own party.

The SDLP argued that they were the major architects of the 1998 Agreement and that the final document was simply the three-stranded process of Northern Ireland, North-South and East-West structures that John Hume had been calling for since early in the process. The Agreement was, in the words of Seamus Mallon, 'Sunningdale for slow learners'. The SDLP argued that Sinn Féin stayed outside the process for most of it, then came in after most of the concessions were won, got some extra concessions, and were then rewarded by the electorate with no recognition given to SDLP achievements.

The SDLP wanted an Assembly having an Executive with legislative and executive functions. They were against devolution of policing and justice as they did not think this would be workable. They were enthusiastic about North-South structures and saw these partly as instruments for practical cooperation and partly necessary to emphasise Irish identity within Northern Ireland. Some were surprised at getting so many of their demands in Strand I - internal Northern Ireland matters - but this was because Unionists were focussed on Strand II issues where they wanted to limit republican demands on North-South bodies.

Other groups at different times made crucial decisions which were vital at the time to keeping the peace process alive. Some examples are:

- The British Government's secret talks with the IRA very early in the process, and their decisions to suspend the Executive on four occasions, each time in their view as a means of keeping the process alive.
- The Dublin Government's decision to hold a referendum which gave up the alleged claim over Northern Ireland, and also their

decision to encourage the US Government to take a positive view of change within the IRA, and Bill Clinton's decision to grant a visa to Gerry Adams in 1994 in the face of vehement British Government opposition.

Each of these decisions was a judgment call by the leaders concerned. If they had got them wrong the process might well have collapsed. Each was difficult because there was often strong opposition from their own side. (In the case of Unionists these divisions were seen in public; among Republicans they were kept behind closed doors). However, because the two communities remained so segregated each misinterpreted what was going on in the other. The result was that few were able to see the cost involved in the changes made by the other side, or that these changes were really meant as a move towards a settlement. Instead, suspicions grew that each side was simply trying to out-manoeuvre the other.

Had the two communities been engaged in dialogue this misinterpretation would have been less likely. The failure to take part in dialogue was a critical factor in the problems which arose.

Behind-the-scenes mediation was critical in the early stages of the process. At that point the only way any of the parties had of knowing what others were open to was through intermediaries. Some of these, like Denis Bradley - later Vice-Chair of the Policing Board - made links between the IRA and the British Government. Many see this link, which predated the Hume-Adams talks, as the most important of the conduits. Others, like Fr Alex Reid and Martin Mansergh, made links between the IRA and the Dublin Government. Civil servants played a key and often hidden role. Protestant clergy played a particular role in meeting Sinn Féin representatives early in the process and convincing them that the blocks to their goals lay as much among Northern Ireland Unionists as with the British Government. They played a similar role in trying to communicate to Loyalists the realities of government policy in the Republic, and their judgement on the reliability of the IRA cessation. The Church intermediaries also played a key role in mediating between republicans, reducing possibilities of feuding and encouraging dialogue which eventually saw the INLA declare a ceasefire.

THE 1998 AGREEMENT: IMPACT AND COMPROMISES
As we have seen the 1998 Agreement was full of ambiguity. Because of this some have asked: was there an Agreement at all, or was it simply

a series of undertakings made between individual parties and the British Government? In other words, did the parties negotiate with the British Government and effectively ignore each other? To argue this is to undersell the Agreement. Some parties negotiated directly with each other, e.g. the UUP and the SDLP, the PUP, Women's Coalition and Sinn Féin. Even if some parties, such as the UUP and Sinn Féin, did not negotiate directly with each other until well into the process, they all agreed to work the institutions, given certain conditions. People disagree as to which parties fulfilled their commitments, but all the parties took part in the Assembly and Executive for protracted periods. The fact that there were difficulties should not detract from the achievement of the Agreement.

As with all political agreements in conflict situations compromise was difficult.

For Republicans it meant putting their dream of unity on the back burner by accepting the principle of consent and committing themselves to giving up violence which had been central to their tactics for decades.

For the SDLP many believe the Agreement was a major reason for their electoral decline, but this was also due to a failure to bring in younger candidates at an earlier stage.

For Unionists it meant facing issues such as the early release of prisoners and the reform of the RUC. Many found these repugnant, some on the basis of their religious beliefs. Others also believed the Agreement weakened the Union, despite the clarity of the clauses on the need for consent. Certainly involvement with Sinn Féin in the absence of unionist satisfaction with decommissioning led to the electoral weakening of the UUP.

The Irish Government gave up its alleged claims to Northern Ireland under Articles II and III of the Republic's Constitution - a key unionist demand for many years. Any change in a written Constitution can be problematic and this proved to be the case when in 2004 the Irish Government held a successful referendum to limit the impact of the new Article II which granted Irish citizenship to children born in Ireland to non-national parents. Southern parties like Fianna Fail also paid a price electorally with the growth of Sinn Féin in the Republic.

The British Government accepted that a decision over a section of its national territory would be made in part by the people of a different State: under the principle of consent they agreed to cooperate with the Irish Government in setting up a United Ireland if the people of Northern Ireland together with the people of the Republic voted for this in referenda.

The Agreement was therefore not easy for any of the participants. Yet the fact that it was made changed politics in Northern Ireland dramatically.

It cemented the relationship between the two Governments.

It opened the possibility among Unionists of power-sharing not only with the SDLP, but also with Republicans. In 2003 the majority of Unionists voted for the DUP, thus rejecting the Agreement. But surveys showed that in the event of Republicans removing arms from the equation the majority of Unionists would be willing to enter government with them.

The Agreement was important in persuading Republicans to stay on cessation and this in turn helped them make political progress among Nationalists and in the Republic.

Cross-border institutions were set up and in time were no longer a contentious issue.

On the other hand the Agreement may also have helped make sectarianism worse. As part of the equality agenda the Police, following Parades Commission decisions, re-routed many Orange parades away from nationalist areas. This brought many interface communities into open and on-going conflict which deeply damaged trust and relationships. Many Protestants felt they were treated unfairly in comparison with Republicans. They felt their sense of Britishness was eroded. This feeling interacted with the general sense of unionist insecurity. In turn this was related to the decline of power and status among Protestants in Ireland as a whole since Catholic Emancipation in 1829. The world as Unionists knew it changed and they saw themselves worse off as a result. Their sense of security about the future was undermined and they feared they were heading to a United Ireland. There were deep divisions between pro- and anti-Agreement people. As the process developed a majority moved to the anti-Agreement position. Even in 1998 only a bare majority of Unionists had supported it.

By the end of the summer of 2004, the Executive had been suspended for almost two years. It remained to be seen if the IRA would or could meet DUP demands for disbandment, and if not, if the unionist community would still support the DUP in the absence of devolution.

OTHER FACTORS IN THE PROCESS

Time to adjust to painful change
One often overlooked factor which helped the peace process was the

length of time it survived. The mere fact of its continued existence bought much needed time. Each passing year that it survived gave people space and time to get used to new and often painful realities. That is why it was so important that it was kept going, even if sometimes it seemed to be on a life-support machine. There were other periods when it was vibrant. But the longer it existed the better people were able to get used to the most uncomfortable changes and also to come to terms with the fact that these changes were not going to be reversed. This did not reduce disagreement but it reduced the emotional content of some disagreement.

For example, cross-border institutions were a major bone of contention for Unionists for many years. Yet when the North-South Ministerial Body was opened in Armagh on 2nd December 1999 there was one solitary protester. The length of the negotiations had given Unionists time to get used to the fact that if there was to be an Agreement it would include North-South bodies. During the negotiations it was eventually accepted that these would be accountable to the Dublin and Stormont Governments (although the London Government took over when the Executive was suspended), but the details probably mattered less than the fact that the emotion surrounding the bodies was gradually reduced. This was in marked contrast to the situation in 1974-5 when the Sunningdale Agreement collapsed, arguably over this issue.

Similarly for many Republicans being part of a Northern Ireland Assembly and accepting ministries in a government devolved from Westminster were at first anathema. Yet over time they too got used to these and quickly gave the impression that they had been in Stormont (in nationalist eyes, that great bastion of unionist power) for years.

The fact that the Executive survived as long as it did was important. It gave Northern Ireland politicians a taste of power. The intervention of the British Government in suspending the Executive at different times was critical. Had they not done this the UUP would have resigned because of their dissatisfaction with the lack of IRA decommissioning. The appointment (or re-appointment) of a First Minister would have required an election within the Assembly. A majority of Unionists would have been necessary for this to succeed and this majority did not exist. By suspending the Executive the British Government were able to restore it without the requirement of an election for a First Minister, and so the process continued. The DUP complained that this was not democratic. The Dublin Government and

Sinn Féin complained that it was not respecting the will of the people of Ireland who had voted for the Assembly and therefore for the Executive in the Agreement. But the rules of the Agreement - which the Dublin Government and Sinn Féin had accepted - allowed for this and if the British Government had not acted as it did the Executive would have collapsed and it would have been much more difficult to keep the process as a whole alive.

The passage of time allowed for the relationship between the UUP and Sinn Féin to thaw at a leadership level, however slowly. This meant, for example, that when the choreography which was part of the UUP-Sinn Féin deal in October 2003 broke down, recriminations between them were much more limited than many expected. Some even wondered if there had been a secret deal between them to allow Trimble go into the election without an agreement so as to help the UUP vote.

The passage of time also helped many Unionists to accept gradually that the IRA cessation, while imperfect, was serious, and that the IRA did not intend to go back to full-scale violence.

David Trimble was able to go into government in the absence of decommissioning on four occasions and survive. Gerry Adams was able to persuade the IRA to decommission on three occasions and survive. These events could not have happened without the passage of a considerable amount of time.

Time was also critical in that it meant judgements could be made especially by David Trimble and Gerry Adams as to when they could make a difficult move. So the longer the IRA remained on cessation the more unlikely it was that they would return to violence. In part this was because they made political gains which they would lose if they returned to violence.

The time factor also helped movement within the DUP. While remaining adamant that they would not go into government or work on committees with Sinn Féin, they did both. They also refused for many years to appear on public platforms with Sinn Féin but in time this also changed as they began to appear in TV studios with them, although never speaking to them directly. When they emerged as the largest party in 2003 they engaged in the subsequent talks on the basis that they wanted a new Agreement. But they knew the two Governments would not accept devolution without the involvement of Sinn Féin. If the DUP wanted devolution they would therefore have to come to some agreement with Republicans. Some characterised the behaviour of the DUP towards Sinn Féin as equivalent to that of the

UUP seven years previously. For its part the DUP said it would only go into government with Sinn Féin when the IRA was abolished.

The length of the process also meant that over the years many ordinary people gradually lost interest in it. This was because of the interminable reports about issues such as decommissioning. It was not that these issues became unimportant to people. They just got tired of talking about them. The boredom factor set in. They got involved in other issues. The result was that politicians got more space to do a deal.

Ambiguous language
The language of the Agreement was ambivalent in many places, as also was that used by many particpants in the wider peace proccss. This helped keep the process alive because different groups could take the interpretation from it which best suited them. An example is the decommissioning clauses. Read literally, all Sinn Féin were required to do was to try to persuade the IRA to decommission by 2000 (two years after the Agreement). Read with the belief that Sinn Féin and the IRA are two sides of the same coin, and also in the light of other clauses in the Agreement requiring the removal of all threat of violence, the IRA were required to have completed decommissioning by 2000.

The fudged language was one of the factors which enabled the IRA not to have to face decommissioning for many years into the process. This was a major problem for Unionists, but arguably had the IRA been faced with this earlier the process would have collapsed. In the end the IRA had to start decommissioning, not because the Agreement required it, but because the UUP required it as a condition of staying in government with Sinn Féin.

At the same time the ambivalence of the Agreement bred distrust because it allowed Republicans to say they were on their way to a United Ireland (a claim which was necessary for their own followers), and this created great fear among Unionists. This fear existed despite the fact that the principle of consent clauses in the Agreement was one of the few places where the language of the document is not ambivalent. These state that no constitutional change can take place without the consent of the majority both of Northern Ireland and of the Republic. Unionists could have pointed to these clauses as greatly strengthening the Union.

Eventually, however, the ambivalent language became counter-productive. An example was the constant denials by Gerry Adams that he was ever in the IRA. Perhaps this is true, but it is hard to find anyone in Northern Ireland who believes it. At one period the denial may have been necessary to avoid arrest but this was hardly the case as the process advanced. A second example was the constant denials by the British Government of charges of collusion, even though considerable sums were paid in out-of-court settlements to those who brought such charges. A third was constant denials by paramilitaries, especially Loyalists, that they were or had been involved in drugs and smuggling rackets. All these undermined credibility in groups which were central to the peace process and this in turn undermined credibility in the process itself. This ambiguity debased political life in Northern Ireland. Because of it many found it difficult to believe much of what any politician said. It was clear that the 'guns and government' issue in the Autumn of 2004 could not be fudged in the same way as previously. But by that time, because the process had survived for so long and because Sinn Féin had made significant gains in the polls, it was easier for Republicans to address the issue.

Democratic structures and international encouragement
The fact that democratic structures had already been established in Northern Ireland and that abuses like the gerrymandering of the early 1970s were removed meant that Republicans could see the possibility of an alternative to violence. Their success at the polls and the correlation between this and moves towards ending violence was also important in helping the Adams' wing persuade others in the movement to support the process. The importance of this should not be overlooked. One of the reasons it has been difficult to make progress in some other conflicts is because of the absence of a democratic option for ex-combatants, and in the Northern Ireland context one of the difficulties faced by Loyalists is their limited political prospects.

The encouragement of the EU, and in particular of the US Government under President Clinton, also helped Republicans to imagine the potential of politics. Part of the US contribution was to reach out to Unionists. The encouragement of President Clinton also helped convince many Republicans that they would be able to make a political impact if they ended violence.

The process was helped by visits to South Africa, the US, and other countries. These allowed for some relationships to develop between individuals, but it also showed how other countries - albeit within very different contexts - had come through an extremely violent past.

Economic changes among UUP and DUP supporters
From the early 1960s manufacturing and textile industries suffered significant decline in Northern Ireland. This can be seen in the dramatic decline in numbers working in Harland and Wolff: down from 35,000 during World War II to approximately 90 permanent and 150 temporary staff by 2004. Much of the business support for the UUP came from groups involved in these industries. As these declined and as the UK became part of a more globalised economy it became less significant economically whether or not Northern Ireland remained part of the UK or joined a United Ireland. In fact, arguably, business people were less concerned about what political party had power, or what the structure of the State was, provided they could get on with making money. In this context they began to encourage Unionists to take part in talks, they supported power-sharing initially with the SDLP, and after the 1994 and 1997 cessations they engaged in dialogue with Sinn Féin. Given the traditional links between the UUP and the business community this was an important change.

The changing economic circumstances also gave a fillip to the DUP as those laid off in traditional Protestant industries resented the changing economic circumstances that saw them decline and Catholics prosper. So they shifted allegiances towards the DUP. At the same time elements of the DUP saw the necessity to modernise and engage with both business people and the Catholic middle class if they were to achieve power.

Lack of symmetry between the parties
An important aspect of the conflict was the lack of symmetry between the parties. Outsiders often focussed on the unionist-nationalist conflict. Yet Republicans saw their conflict as being with the British Government and in the early stages tended to see Unionists as simply pawns of the British. It took time for them to realise that the blocks to their ambitions lay in Belfast as much as in London. Unionists saw Republicans as a threat but their answer to the threat was to focus on British responses to Republicans. The two parties did not have face-to-face negotiations until after the Agreement.

At times, because of the threat of renewed republican violence the British Government focussed on Sinn Féin demands and paid less attention to those of Unionists. At other times, when they feared that the UUP would pull down the process, they did the opposite. Each party therefore pulled at the strings of the British Government and were often focussed on it rather than on each other. At the same time,

Unionists were more likely to be obsessed with Republicans than *vice versa*.

As the process developed and after Northern Ireland politicians had experienced devolution, it became clear to both Unionists and Republicans that they could not continue with devolution without the consent of each other. When the DUP and Sinn Féin defeated the UUP and the SDLP respectively in the 2003 election it was obvious that any devolved government would have to be agreed between the two leading parties.

The two Governments did not act as disinterested outsiders (although they liked to present this as their stance). In practice their role varied from aggressively championing one of the internal groups to working together in challenging one or both. Gradually throughout the process they moved more towards the latter position.

Who were the parties to the conflict?
During the peace process there was a gradual movement from seeing the conflict as a clash of identities to seeing it as a double minority problem. This in turn led to an emphasis on the need for status, respect and economic improvement. In the early stages Nationalists successfully presented themselves as the more marginalised. In later years Unionists, especially Loyalists, argued that it was they and not Nationalists who were the more excluded.

The double minority thesis maintains not only that both Unionists and Nationalists saw themselves as a minority, but also that each had an ambivalent relationship with the London or Dublin Government, and that these had an up and down relationship with each other. One advantage of this approach is that it avoids the temptation to see the conflict as simply one between Unionists and Nationalists. The British and Irish Governments were also involved, as was the US. The importance of asking who the protagonists are can be seen in the Middle East: one would make a profound mistake by assuming the conflict there is only between Israeli Jews and Palestinians. The US, and to a lesser extent, surrounding Arab States and the EU, are all heavily involved, and they see their own interests at stake in the conflict.

Lack of dialogue among segregated groups
A major problem in the process was that segregation not only persisted but deepened after the 1998 Agreement. The process for the most part was conducted between the two Governments and the political parties. When the British Government intervened at a local level, for example

at Drumcree in Portadown or with other interface issues, it faced a dilemma. Local issues, such as disputed parades, were symptoms of, and related to, the wider conflict. Secondly, they were often win-lose situations: either a parade went ahead or it did not. It was highly unlikely that locals would agree an outcome given that the rest of Northern Ireland was bitterly divided and given also that issues such as parades were highly emotive. There were exceptions to this rule, such as in Londonderry, where local residents and Apprentice Boys eventually worked out a way to handle the parades issue.

Divisions between Unionists and Nationalists were made worse because on the one hand Republicans believed it was in their interests to highlight what they saw as progress towards a United Ireland and to hold out for further gains on issues such as policing, while the DUP highlighted the threat of Republicans. Both the DUP and Sinn Féin gained electorally from these tactics. They were then left with a problem: if they wanted devolved government they had to win the consent of the other side. They also had to get the consent of their own followers. Given that many had voted for the DUP on the grounds that they would prefer Direct Rule in all circumstances to seeing Sinn Féin in government, the DUP was left with the question of how it could sell any deal which included Sinn Féin to its electorate.

This highlighted the vast need for dialogue among non-party-political groups. Without this it was difficult to see how the political parties could get the space to make compromises, even if they wanted to do so. During the process some in the political parties had gained considerable new experience of dealing with former enemies. This was especially true of those who were negotiators. While others in the parties were not directly involved nonetheless they still learnt something about the other side from what their negotiators said. However, the wider public had no direct experience of the process. Most had never discussed politics or their differences with people from the other community. In this context the need for dialogue, and the lack of attention paid to it, was glaring.

The ineffectiveness of violence
Many in Northern Ireland, both Unionists and Nationalists, believe that Republicans achieved what they did because of violence. Many Loyalists - and probably some Unionists - also believe that a major influence in bringing the IRA to a cessation was loyalist murders of ordinary Catholics. Others believe that security-force violence successfully blocked the IRA. These beliefs are almost certainly wrong. Further, the existence of these beliefs makes it more likely that groups

will resort to violence in the future.

As Unionists saw it, before the cessation Republicans were officially seen by the Government as criminals. If they were arrested and convicted they were sent to jail. During the peace process that all changed. Republicans were let out of jail, they were seen by the Government as legitimate politicians, one Sinn Féin member became the Minister for Education and another the Minister for Health and there was even talk of Gerry Adams getting the Nobel Peace prize. If Republicans did not get all this through violence how else did they get it?

For Republicans, a commitment to violence as a means of expelling the British from Northern Ireland was always important. So it was difficult for them to entertain the idea that violence was not central to their achievements.

In reality, however, the violence of Republicans was the biggest block to their political progress (Unionists collapsed the Executive on four occasions because of the 'guns and government' issue). Before the ceasefire they had great difficulty in persuading anyone outside their ranks to talk to them. There were contacts with the British Government, some Roman Catholic priests kept in touch with them and the Hume-Adams talks took place. But the purpose of these was to persuade Republicans to end violence. The US government refused Republicans visas (with the notable exception of Clinton in 1994, and that was because he hoped it would help Adams get a ceasefire). Because of the violence the Catholic community (the majority of whom always opposed violence) were bitterly divided. As well as this, violence had a particularly negative impact on community work in more deprived areas, and the skills and efforts of many talented individuals, instead of going into community and economic enterprises, were focussed on killing people. More Catholics were killed by republican paramilitaries than by the security forces and Loyalists combined. The violence alienated many Nationalists, especially in the South, from the idea of a United Ireland. It increased unionist fears of a United Ireland, of Catholics in general, and of Republicans in particular. Together with State and loyalist violence republican violence helped the growth of sectarianism, it reduced tolerance and increased segregation. It left a legacy by giving future generations a role model they could follow, and it left open the argument that others who were dissatisfied with their political situation had as much right as Republicans to turn to violence to bring about change.

There was one other impact of republican violence: while violence

was on-going it was a block to negotiations and therefore to any
progress Republicans wished to make politically. The British
Government frequently put the argument to the Dublin Government
that there was no point in their making concessions because these
would not end the violence. However, while violence *before* the
cessation was a block to republican progress, *after* the cessation the
threat of returning to violence was effective as a means to extract
concessions. One can argue, therefore, that the threat would have been
ineffective had it not been preceded with actual violence. Without this
threat how many concessions would Sinn Féin have failed to gain? It
is not possible to answer this question but a guess is that they would
have failed to win some changes in policing. How much difference
these changes would make to policing on the ground remains to be
seen. It would be difficult to argue that they were worth the pain and
division caused by the violence.

On other occasions Republicans were helped by Unionists. In
response to demands for decommissioning they were able to ask 'What
will you give us in return?' It was always a matter of judgment as to
whether republican threats were real, and, if so, whether making
concessions would lead to progress or simply to further demands. The
Unionists' perception was that the Government undermined
democratic politics by giving into threats. The perception of
Republicans, however, was that what they got were not concessions at
all but human rights from which Unionists as well as everyone else
benefited.

Loyalists argued that their violence was reactive: when the IRA
stopped being a threat to the State they would in turn stop. Yet loyalist
violence between 1997 and 2004 was far greater than that of
Republicans. Further, unionist politicians constantly focussed on
republican violence and tended only to mention loyalist violence as an
afterthought, or in order to appear balanced. While many Loyalists
believe their violence was important in persuading Republicans to
move to a ceasefire, Republicans deny this and point instead to the
political potential they saw in a ceasefire as being more important.

The security forces always maintained that they only killed people
in self-defence. There have been too many questionable incidents for
this to be credibly maintained - examples are the killings investigated
by John Stalker, and the Pat Finucane, Billy Wright and Rosemary
Nelson murders. Presumably those who ordered security-force killings
believed they were effective. In reality they gave the republican
movement martyrs and reinforced the beliefs of those who found the
State unjust. To that extent they were ineffective. In practice

intelligence work by the security forces probably made a far greater impact on the IRA than any extra-judicial killings which the security forces carried out or supported. It can, however, be argued that by supporting loyalist killings the State helped promote the perception of the conflict as a nasty, sectarian conflict, which made it more difficult for Republicans to present it as a glorious struggle for national independence.

Others point out that looking for rational arguments for violence make no sense because violence in practice does not break out as a result of a commitment to some ideology. Often it is not part of a coherent plan. Rather it develops in different places as an immediate response to a perceived attack, without anyone seeing the long-term consequences and only gradually turns into a coherent movement. From this standpoint it is useless to argue about the achievements or otherwise of violence. Instead one should focus on the conditions which made violence more or less likely. One element which increased the likelihood of republican violence was their interpretation of Irish history. They focussed on the physical-force tradition to show that there had been a centuries-long violent struggle for Irish freedom. Others would differ and point out that 19th century Irish history was dominated by the figures of Daniel O'Connell and Charles Stewart Parnell - both of whom were constitutionalists (although Parnell was not averse to the threat of force on occasion) - and that the 1916 Rising was initially supported by very few. The real change in Irish history, in this view, came with the transfer of land from landlords to peasants. Michael Davitt was the most prominent figure in this struggle, and although a member of the Fenians, his success was due not to violence, but to his combined political work with Parnell.

Whatever view one takes of this issue, the fact is that one of the models available to northern Catholics in 1969 was the 1916 Rising and that was the model a minority adopted. This was in marked contrast to the route chosen by African-Americans in the US, the majority of whom followed the path of Martin Luther King in dealing with the race issue.

For their part, Loyalists in using force were following the example of the British who took the island of Ireland by force (helped by many Irish people), and both force and the threat of force were central in ensuring that Northern Ireland was separated politically from the rest of the island in 1920.

One result of the violence, and the widespread belief that it led to political progress, was that it made it more difficult to persuade young people that violence was not the only, or natural, or best way to resolve problems. This was made worse by the glorification by paramilitaries of what they had done in the past.

Factors in other peace processes
In most peace processes a number of tasks need to be dealt with for the peace to develop and last. Among these are:
- Disarming, demobilizing and integrating ex-combatants.
- Policing.
- Dealing with trauma, bereavement and mental health.
- Dealing with those exiled by paramilitaries and people on the run from courts.
- Finding a way to deal with the past.
- Getting agreement about the rule of law.
- Promoting human rights.
- Agreeing a Constitution.

It is worth noting that, unlike other countries, there were a number of problems which Northern Ireland did *not* have to face, e.g., clearing landmines, ensuring a supply of food, building roads, the need to build an infrastructure of houses, power and transport, or the need to deal with large numbers of refugees - except at the times like the loyalist feuds on the Shankill Road in Belfast when a considerable number were made homeless and also in the early stages of the Troubles.

The Northern Ireland situation was therefore incomparably better than that of many third-world countries facing a legacy of conflict. In Sudan, for example, in 2004 there were about 4 million internally displaced people, up to 2 million refugees abroad, and large-scale killings.

In a study of the implementation of agreements in sixteen countries between 1980 and 1997, Steve Stedman of Stanford University lists a number of factors which he believes make the implementation of a peace agreement more difficult (Paper presented at the 8th Glencree Summer School 24th August 2001):
1. If there are more than two parties involved.
2. If the agreement was coerced.
3. If there is a collapsed State, as in Somalia where there was no government and the State had ceased functioning.
4. If one or more of the parties wants to set up a separate State.
5. If there is a large number of combatants to be demobilised. (Stedman arbitrarily set a figure of 50,000 combatants as a threshold of difficulty).

6. If there are spoilers. (These are leaders or factions that see peace as something opposed to their worldview, power, or interests, and who are willing to use violence against those who want peace).
7. If there are spoils (valuable easily marketable commodities like timber or diamonds. Some estimate that rebels in Sierra Leone earned more than $100 million a month from the diamond trade by continuing the civil war).
8. If there are hostile neighbours.

He listed two factors which make implementation easier:
1. Economic interdependence among adversaries, as in South Africa where black labour and white capitalists realised they needed each other.
2. The existence of a robust civil society with plenty of information exchange and dialogue, together with an independent media.

He suggested that the following factors in order of importance are most likely to lead to a positive outcome:
1. Demoblisation of combatants.
2. Building local capacity to sustain peace.
3. Reforming the Police and the Judiciary.
4. Assisting the internally displaced.
5. Human rights.
6. Disarmament.

Of these he concluded that demobilization of combatants was the most important in the short term. Disarmament was not a priority: in his view if paramilitaries are demobilised and if they are convinced that they can have a future without violence, then disarmament will follow. In the long-term the two most important factors were building local capacity to sustain peace and reforming the Police and Judiciary. Human rights as a separate category was down the list. Why? Because countries which intervene in disputes to bring about a resolution are often not willing to spend the time and resources needed to build up human rights. 'We recommend that if you care about human rights, then you need to think about human rights as being a part of all of the above six concerns and which has to be worked at from the bottom up through building local capacity.' (S. Stedman, 'Reflections on Implementing Peace Agreements', Community Dialogue video tape, 2002).

It is worth noting here that the central fault line in the Northern

Ireland peace process is between those who have been willing to work with paramilitaries apparently moving to end violence and those who were not. Those who were willing to work with paramilitaries stressed that moving away from violence is a process and takes time. In Northern Ireland most Nationalists were willing to give Republicans time to move towards politics and in 2003 the majority of Nationalists voted for Sinn Féin, even though the IRA was still active. The unionist side was sharply divided between the UUP who went into government with Sinn Féin on the understanding that paramilitary activity would end in the not-too-distant future and the DUP who said they would never share power with Republicans while the IRA existed, but who, despite this, took their seats in the Cabinent when the Executive was up and running.

CONCLUSION

By any account the 1998 Agreement was a transforming moment in Irish history, but this is perhaps more easily understood because of changes in the nationalist and republican communities than among Unionists. The most critical change was that as a direct result of the Agreement Republicans moved into devolved government in Northern Ireland. For many Unionists this was a nightmare as they feared that republican violence would continue. In fact it did continue, but at a vastly reduced level. Further, the contradictions between being part of a government while at the same time linked to an active paramilitary group became more stark for Republicans as the process proceeded.

For Unionists the Agreement involved a major readjustment because Republicans successfully presented themselves to the world as former paramilitaries who were now committed to constitutional politics. Unionist criticisms in this light seemed negative and ungenerous and they had a hard time presenting their case. They were slower than Republicans to learn some basic media skills. Further, if Republicans were economical with the truth in downplaying on-going IRA activity, Unionists also presented a simplistic picture of the conflict in which they were simply law-abiding citizens and Republicans were all criminals.

Had the IRA not agreed to a cessation Republicans would not have been involved in the peace process. There probably would have been a power-sharing deal between the UUP and the SDLP against the background of continued violence. Many more would have lost their lives. However, many, while glad that the IRA declared a cessation, pointed out that Republicans killed nearly 2000 people during the

Troubles but then acted as if they were the only victims. They demanded human rights and investigations into security force abuses, and they condemned corruption in Southern politics, against a background in which the IRA were still active and were accused of on-going involvement in punishment beatings and smuggling rackets. Loyalists complained about being marginalised in the process, but between 1999 and 2002 (inclusive) the International Monitoring Commission report of 20 April 2004 attributed forty killings to them (Republicans allegedly killed fifteen in the same period). According to security-force sources Loyalists were still involved in major drug rackets in 2004. Both Republicans and Loyalists respond to such charges by saying that they should not all be tarred with the same brush and that only a minority are involved in these activities.

The violence of both Loyalists and Republicans undoubtedly harmed the peace process. At the same time leaders among them at different times played positive roles in its development. The role of the two Governments was, however, the critical factor in setting the framework within which the peace process developed. This remains the permanent aspect of both the 1985 and 1998 Agreements. Even if the Northern Ireland parties fail to resolve their differences the Agreements between the two Governments will continue. The principle of consent will remain in place. Progress on human rights legislation will continue to the extent that this is in the interests of the two Governments (and public opinion can influence this). Northern Ireland, critically, will continue to be represented in Europe by the British Government primarily, although Northern Ireland MEPs will also be able to play a role. In the light of this it would therefore be wrong to think the Agreement failed because the Northern Ireland parties could not agree about an Executive. That was only part of the Agreement. The wider measures remained in place. By the middle of 2004 it was unclear whether or not the Executive would be restored. Nor was it clear whether or not Unionists and Nationalists would commit themselves together to creating a new Northern Ireland, or remain in separate and opposing camps.

This section has looked at what helped to bring the peace process about. But getting to the Agreement was only part of the battle. Bedding it down, helping it to survive and implementing it were just as problematic. The process was frequently stuck. In the next section we look at the major issues in 2004, just after the DUP and Sinn Féin had been successful in the 2003 election.

2

A Sulky Stalemate?
Blocks in 2004

'GUNS AND GOVERNMENT'

INTRODUCTION

What were the major blocks to the peace process in the summer of 2004? It is worth looking at this question because it shows how more general issues impacted on the process at a particular point. Further, it is useful to look back to see how these issues were overcome. At the time each of them seemed particularly difficult. Yet, at the end of the summer of that year, despite the fact that the DUP had campaigned in the 2003 election on the basis that they were the true Unionists who had not compromised with Republicans, the mood music between them and Sinn Féin suggested a deal was more rather than less likely.

Throughout much of the process the dominant issue was known in shorthand as 'guns and government': Unionists refused to go into government with Sinn Féin on the grounds that the IRA had not decommissioned. Republicans said the guns would disappear when politics was working. By the end of 2003, five years after the Agreement was signed, the Executive had collapsed four times primarily because of this issue.

The issue was the focus for several different problems:
- Deep unionist resentment at Republicans being in government without any - as they saw it - repentance for past crimes.
- A lack of confidence between the UUP and Sinn Féin: the UUP believed that Republicans would avoid decommissioning forever if they could get away with it. Sinn Féin believed the UUP wanted to exclude them from government.
- The lack of confidence was fed by rows over three critical issues:
  - Decommissioning,
  - Continued paramilitary activity
  - Policing.

In this chapter we will try to unpack these issues.

COSTLY CONCESSIONS

The divisions between Unionists and Nationalists over decommissioning, paramilitary violence and policing between 1998 and 2004 were deep. Nonetheless progress was made, and during the process all the major parties changed their position. Before the 1994 cessation the British Government had said they would not talk to Sinn Féin while violence was on-going. In March 1995 Secretary of State Patrick Mayhew introduced a further condition by insisting that decommissioning preceded talks. Yet in practice the Government not only talked to Republicans but approved a devolved government with Sinn Féin included while IRA activity, albeit at a low level, continued.

The British Government was criticised on many occasions by Republicans for destabilising the institutions by giving in to unionist demands and suspending the Assembly. The Dublin Government publicly shared this view on several occasions. Yet the rules of the Agreement meant that the Assembly could not function without cross-community consent: both Unionists and Nationalists had a veto. The British Government also bent the rules to keep the institutions going. On 15 July 1999 Seamus Mallon resigned as Deputy First Minister. The Assembly was subsequently suspended. When it was reinstated, a motion should have been put to it to re-appoint Mallon. This motion would not have passed because it needed the support of the majority of both Unionists and Nationalists, and the Unionists would have rejected it. Because of this the Government decided that Mallon had never resigned in the first place and therefore did not need to be re-appointed. Had the Government not acted as it did, it is difficult to see how the Assembly could have been revived. Some argue that this might have led to negotiations between the DUP and Sinn Féin with an earlier resolution of difficulties. On the other hand, the fact that the Assembly survived as long as it did gave Northern Ireland politicians experience of government. This certainly helped the slow process by which the Agreement survived for as long as it did. However, the clear breach of the rules of the Assembly in order to achieve a particular outcome favoured by the Government undermined the confidence of many Unionists in the integrity of the process and made anti-agreement voters feel more justified in their position.

The UUP also said it would not go into government with Sinn Féin until decommissioning was complete but then did so on four separate occasions.

Republicans said they would not decommission 'one ounce' of weapons but then did so on three different occasions.

Sinn Féin-UUP Progress in 2003

In the autumn of 2003 it looked as if there could be a deal between David Trimble and Gerry Adams. This was helped by several factors. Interface violence had been relatively subdued during the summer and both Republicans and Loyalists had worked to ensure this. So also had many community groups. Secondly, Republicans came up with a formula to end violence more advanced than that of April 2003. Both these factors strengthened unionist confidence about republican intentions.

For their part Republicans saw David Trimble confront Jeffrey Donaldson at the Ulster Council meeting of 8 September 2003 and win, and this helped convince them that Unionists were serious about wanting stable political institutions provided the arms issue could be dealt with. It also provided evidence that Trimble was still in the driving seat of the UUP and that he was likely to be able to deliver his side of any deal they made with him. They were further encouraged by the UUP's willingness to consider devolution of policing, which opened up the possibility of a Sinn Féin Minister in charge of policing.

In the event Unionists rejected what seems to have been a major act of IRA decommissioning in November 2003 because they saw it as insufficiently transparent. At the time this was seen as a major blow for the peace process. It might have been different if General de Chastelain - head of the body overseeing decommissioning - had been able to announce that the IRA had given him a complete list of their inventory, that they had undertaken to complete decommissioning within one year, and that he was personally confident both about the accuracy of the information he had received and that the IRA would do what they said they would do. That might have been sufficient to swing a majority of unionist voters behind the UUP, but such an outcome would have been highly uncertain, given the extent of unionist alienation. In any case the IRA was unable to deliver anything like this clarity. Sinn Féin would be in a much better position to do so after they emerged clearly as the strongest nationalist party in the 2004 election.

Ironically, the breakdown in the 2003 negotiations may have led to an even better outcome - at least in terms of the political process: the DUP and Sinn Féin emerged from the election as the strongest parties. Both wanted devolved government and they needed each other to achieve this.

Byron Bland and Lee Ross from Stanford University have made the point that a critical factor in a peace process is to face what they call the 'peace question': to distinguish aims a group wants and *can* achieve without the consent of the other side, from those they want but *cannot* achieve without the consent of the other. (The issue was discussed in the three year study on 'Reconciliation and Dialogue' which Community Dialogue made with Stanford Center on Conflict and Negotiation). For much of the process both Unionists and Republicans believed that they could get what they wanted without the other side. So Unionists focussed on excluding Republicans, Republicans focussed on the British Government and tended to ignore Unionists. However, as the process developed, and especially as both sides experienced devolved government and enjoyed it, the extent increased to which they had to take account of the needs of the other side in order to achieve their own ends. There would be no agreement without sorting out the decommissioning issue in a way that both parties could live with.

THE AGREEMENT ON DECOMMISSIONING
The decommissioning section of the Agreement was vague and aspirational. It was precisely for this reason that leading UUP negotiator Jeffrey Donaldson left the Talks on the night before the Agreement in 1998. Participants affirmed 'their commitment to the total disarmament of all paramilitary organisations'. They also undertook to continue to work with the Independent International Commission on Decommissioning and 'to use any influence they may have, to achieve the decommissioning of all paramilitary arms within two years'. Elsewhere in the Agreement the parties renounced the use of violence or the threat of violence as a political weapon.

ARGUMENTS FOR AND AGAINST DECOMMISSIONING
Sinn Féin said that they had used all their influence to bring about disarmament, that the way to achieve decommissioning was to get stable political institutions in place and that the IRA were not a party to the Agreement.

For their part, Unionists pointed out that as far back as 1997 Sinn Féin had accepted the Mitchell Principles under which decommissioning was supposed to take place during the Talks, and that it was nonsense to talk of Sinn Féin using all their influence on the IRA since they and the IRA were one and the same thing.

Nationalists asked why Unionists insisted on decommissioning when arms could be replaced after decommissioning, and they argued that what mattered was that guns were silenced, not decommissioned. For Republicans and many other Nationalists the constant focus on decommissioning was seen as a demand for surrender. Because Unionists maintained their demands despite three separate acts of IRA decommissioning, many took the view that they would never be satisfied. It was also suggested that buried arms rust so they were no threat, an argument dismissed by General de Chastelain, who pointed out that arms kept in proper conditions would not rust.

Unionists argued that they were not using decommissioning as an underhand means of getting a republican surrender. Rather they needed it as a confidence-building mechanism to show that the violence was over. Further, they asked, if the violence was really over, why did Republicans want to hang on to their guns?

Unionists often misinterpreted Republicans by focussing more on what Republicans said than on what they did. For example, they often saw the failure of Sinn Féin to condemn the IRA in the early days of the process as a sign that they were open to returning to violence, when in fact the verbal ambivalence was necessary to keep their more militant followers on-side. At the same time the decision by Sinn Féin to accept places in the new Assembly was, within the context of republican history, one of the most powerful statements imaginable that the war really was over. To become Ministers in a British Government, to take a pledge of office to 'serve all the people of Northern Ireland' (not 'the people of Ireland'), these actions - for those who knew the republican movement - were far greater evidence of the war being over than any decommissioning of easily-replaceable arms. However, the continued involvement of the IRA in violence made it even more difficult to convince Unionists that republican changes were genuine.

POSITIVE AND NEGATIVE CONTRIBUTIONS TO THE PROCESS

Both the UUP and Sinn Féin made positive and negative contributions to keeping the process alive in the period up to the fourth collapse of the Executive in October 2002. Yet even the apparently negative contributions may have had a positive impact in the long run, either because they helped keep doubters involved, or because they pressed the other side to make a move which ultimately was necessary for the process to survive. The UUP went into government four times while the IRA was still active, but then also collapsed the Executive over decommissioning. Republicans kept the IRA moving towards peace, they called cessations of violence, and they carried out three acts of decommissioning. On the other hand they also failed to realise that David Trimble was unable to remain in Government with them without moves which effectively built up unionist confidence that the IRA were going out of business. The tragedy was that the three IRA acts of decommissioning seemed to be substantial - but the 'seemed to be' in that last phrase left too much ambiguity for a distrustful unionist community.

THE IMPACT OF VIOLENCE ON THE PROCESS

Assessments of the IRA cessation
Many Unionists believed the IRA cessation was tactical. This seemed to mean that after Sinn Féin had extracted as many political concessions as they could the IRA would go back to violence. Another version was that violence would be carried on unofficially by dissident Republicans with the tacit consent of the IRA and/or with overlaps between dissident and IRA membership. Then the violence would be used by Sinn Féin to extract more concessions in the talks.

These fears were supported by some public security-force assessments which pointed out that in the period after 1997 the IRA continued to recruit, gather intelligence, target security force members, and were engaged in smuggling and other crime. Against these views, the vast majority of people who knew the republican movement well believed that the IRA's moves towards politics were irreversible, especially in the light of Republicans taking their seats in the Assembly and the Executive, moves which were directly opposed to their previous ideology. These assessments did not focus on IRA criminal activity or on their control of local areas, or so-called punishment beatings. Rather, they pointed to the belief that the organisation's violence against the British was over. They also believed that the supporters of Gerry Adams within the movement were focussed on practical improvements for Republicans living in Northern Ireland by working through political structures. While this would involve North-South structures it would not lead to a United Ireland in the short term. From a republican point of view this was a momentous change.

The public thus faced conflicting assessments of the reliability of the IRA cessation. In each case the views were communicated by proxies: the security force views were mediated by the Government or unionist politicians, the more hopeful view by people in the nationalist community who were clearly opposed to violence but who had maintained contact with Republicans in the hope of moving them towards politics.

Few Unionists were in a position to make informed judgements about the reliability of IRA statements because most of them had not engaged in dialogue privately or publicly with Republicans.

Republicans for their part were ambivalent about violence. 'TUAS', the acronym used in internal IRA documents was open to two different interpretations: Sinn Féin's nationalist allies were told it stood for 'Totally UnArmed strategy' while activists were told it stood for a 'Tactical Use of Armed Struggle (cf. Ed Moloney, *A Secret History of the IRA*, Penguin, 2002, p. 423). One meant the end of violence, the other meant a tactical pause, which was precisely what many Unionists feared. TUAS in the sense of 'Totally UnArmed Struggle' went against what many Republicans saw as the essence of the movement. Had Gerry Adams stated this as his goal too early in the process he would not have survived as leader of Sinn Féin.

Levels of loyalist and republican violence
The April 2004 International Monitoring Commission's Report found that:
- In the period 1999-2002 Loyalists killed 40 people, Republicans killed 15.
- Between 1 January 2003 and 29 February 2004 12 people were murdered by paramilitaries, 8 by Loyalists (5 by the UDA), 2 by Republicans, 2 others by unknown groups.
- In the same period Loyalists shot 123 and assaulted 116 people, Republicans shot 66 and assaulted 56.
- The Report said that Loyalists are 'now responsible for markedly higher levels of violence than Republicans: about three quarters of the murders, nearly twice as many shootings and over twice as many assaults since 1 January 2003'.
- The IRA 'are highly active in paramilitary shootings short of murder'. They are 'not presently involved in attacks on the security forces'. The Commission believed the IRA can turn attacks on and off and that they turned them off during the Assembly elections. They also believe it was they who attacked Robert Tohill, in Belfast in February 2004. (The Police rescued Tohill from the back of a van and charged four men with his attempted kidnapping).

In press reports in March 2004 the Chief Constable, Hugh Orde, said that both Loyalists and Republicans were responsible for punishment beatings and that Loyalists were involved in drug peddling. Republican beatings were mostly carried out by the IRA, not dissident Republicans. The head of the Assets Recovery Agency, Alan McQuillan, said the IRA was involved in smuggling fuel and a figure of £200 million as the amount involved 'does not seem to me to be an unreasonable estimate'. The Dublin Government accused the IRA of being involved in crime in Dublin docks and on the Border.

Sinn Féin responded to these charges by saying they were willing to discuss paramilitarism, but not if the focus was exclusively on Republicans.

Caution should be exercised in judging claims by the security forces. Charges of membership of the IRA against the four men in the Tohill case were dropped three days later when they were brought to court. Police sources said they had overlooked the fact that the IRA was not a 'specified' organisation as it was 'on ceasefire', but nonetheless insisted the organisation was responsible for the attempted kidnapping of Robert Tohill, a view later supported by the International Monitoring Commission. The PSNI in October 2002 had staged a major raid on Sinn Féin offices in Stormont. The media had been tipped off in advance. Several computer disks were lifted. Allegations of a major spying ring on the British, Irish and US Governments were made. Yet when the cases came to court most of the major charges were dropped. The Stormont spying case was the immediate trigger for David Trimble pulling the UUP out of the Executive. The Robert Tohill case led to him pulling his party out of the Review of the Agreement.

Against this it is clear that punishment beatings and smuggling operations took place in republican areas. This meant that either these areas had been taken over by dissidents which was extremely unlikely, or else that Republicans were overseeing, tolerating or benefiting from these incidents.

It was certainly the case that the majority of paramilitary incidents between 1998 and 2004 were carried out by Loyalists rather than Republicans. Yet Unionists charged with reason that there was also one major difference between the two: Sinn Féin will be in government if the Executive is restored. From a constitutional point of view that made republican violence much more significant. There is a basic contradiction between holding government office in a democratic State and being linked to a private army. Accepting office implies a recognition of the State, especially in the light of the principle of consent clauses in the Agreement. For a State to function properly the government needs to have control over legitimate force. By the beginning of 2004 it was clear that both the UUP and the DUP would not return to devolved government with Sinn Féin until this issue was resolved.

In July 2004 Chief Constable Hugh Orde said that in his view IRA violence was at an end and that they would not return to it.

Paramilitarism

The 'guns and government' issue was a symptom of the problem of paramilitaries which in turn was a legacy of the violence. Paramilitary organisations were deeply embedded in communities, mostly working-class, in Northern Ireland. Members had a mixture of reasons:

- They saw violence as the only way to achieve their political goals.
- They liked the power they held over the community through the threat of force.
- Sufficient people in the local community felt they needed them to defend them against paramilitaries from the other side, or against the security forces.
- People wanted them to police their area against car thieves and other forms of social crime.

Paramilitaries by definition are not democrats. They are not elected by their communities, they are at best marginally accountable to them, and some either direct drugs dealings and smuggling operations or else live off the proceeds of these by allowing them to operate.

Political parties linked to paramilitaries are tainted by what paramilitaries do. Many members of these parties who had no connection with the paramilitaries argued that they should not all be tarred with the same brush. 'Arrest the criminals', they said, 'but don't accuse us of crime'. In fact it was inevitable that members of organisations were associated by the public with crimes committed even by a minority of members. Besides, political parties associated with paramilitary groups by definition have a tolerance of the paramilitaries that others find unacceptable. Ultimately, there were only two options for those who wanted not to be tainted with paramilitarism: split from the paramilitaries or successfully transform the organisations.

Transforming paramilitary organisations was bound to be difficult. Those who chose this route were used and abused: on the one hand the

Police and other bodies asked for their help to keep the peace during times of tension. On the other they, along with active paramilitaries, were blamed for the wrongs committed by the organisation.

As with so much else in the peace process, there were nuances and ironies which should be explored about this issue. It was only the IRA which could effectively deal with republican paramilitaries. It was only they who could decide whether protection, smuggling and drug rackets would continue or not in republican areas. It was probably only they who could decide whether the case of Gareth O'Connor who disappeared in South Armagh in May 2003 and was still missing in the Autumn of 2004, would be resolved or not.

Similarly it was only Loyalists who could decide whether or not their rackets would continue.

The battle to make paramilitarism a thing of the past needs to be waged on a number of fronts:

- Politically, to show paramilitaries that they can be included on an equal opportunity basis with everyone else in society if they give up violence.
- By local communities deciding that there are other and better ways to get security and policing.
- By the Police focussing on law-breaking.
- By the Assets Recovery Agency ensuring that crime pays less.
- By paramilitaries and others working at interfaces to develop and maintain communication.
- By political parties connected to paramilitaries facing the contradiction of wanting to be involved in democratic politics and to enjoy human rights while at the same time being connected to self-appointed groups involved in criminal activity.

All these approaches need to work simultaneously.

In simplistic public debate the paramilitaries were seen as the bad guys. In fact many individuals in paramilitary organisations played key positive roles in limiting the violence of their organisations and in moving their organisations away from crime. Many ex-prisoners gave important leadership in persuading young people not to get involved in violence. Precisely because of their history of violence these ex-prisoners had street credibility greater than any outsider. At different stages of the peace process the decision of prisoners to support it was crucial.

The question arises then: will paramilitaries continue to exist in Northern Ireland in 2010, 2015, 2030? The guns will continue to exist, because the US, the UK, and other countries will still manufacture them, and so people in Northern Ireland will be able to get them. The attractions of crime will not go away. Nor will the attraction of power and status which can go along with belonging to a paramilitary group. People in interface areas and others will continue to be afraid and the Police will not be able to respond effectively to all calls. The history of 35 years of conflict means people have got used to violence, and street violence in general in the Western world increased in the last quarter of the last century.

Paramilitarism is far more common in working-class than in middle-class areas. In this respect Northern Ireland is similar to other countries where more deprived areas bear the brunt of drug crime. The reasons are obvious: in areas of greater relative poverty options are drastically reduced. That is why fewer people from deprived areas finish second-level education or go to university, have more hospital admissions, have a greater rate of mental health problems, and die younger. When one adds a history of paramilitary activity and when this is linked to the emotional appeal of either British or Irish nationalism, the attraction of paramilitarism for some is obvious. A fifteen year old youth doing badly at school with poor prospects is going to be tempted by the wealth and status apparently enjoyed by paramilitaries in his community, especially if he can be led to believe he is doing something for his country. As always, social conditioning makes it more or less likely that people will turn to violence.

All this suggests that paramilitarism will continue to be a major problem in Northern Ireland.

People in Northern Ireland could do something about this, but only with concerted programmes in which Unionists and Nationalists worked together on education, job creation, cultural analysis, citizenship and other issues, and if there was a devolved political system with good links to the Community Sector.

In other conflict situations demobilization of ex-combatants has been an important factor in moves towards peace. It is difficult for some who have been members of paramilitary groups and who have thereby had access to power and/or wealth, with the self-esteem this gives to some, to give it up. It helps if alternatives are available. That is precisely why many former paramilitaries have set up community groups which not only give new outlets to their talents but also benefit their local community. If the Government fails to fund groups in which paramilitaries have found ways to make positive contributions to society then not only will they lose the new contribution being made by the paramilitaries, the Government will also make it harder for paramilitaries to persuade their colleagues to go the way of peace.

At the same time public funding of groups associated with paramilitaries cannot go on forever. A transition period has a beginning and an end. The second IRA ceasefire was in 1997. Seven years later they were still in business. How long would this continue? Loyalists, despite their ceasefires, had continued killing both Catholics and each other. Republicans said arms would disappear when the context was 'right'. Even those who accepted a transition period was necessary dismissed this because it could mean anything. The question remained of how long the transition would last and no satisfactory answer had been given.

As can be seen from the above in 2004 we remained deeply ambivalent about the role of paramilitaries in Northern Ireland. To some extent this ambivalence was inevitable after a highly destructive and painfully violent conflict. It also arose because paramilitaries were able to touch on values which are emphasised by the State: patriotism and sacrifice on behalf of the people. In part it came about because many avoided tough questions about the legitimacy and accountability of paramilitary groups. Many paramilitaries argued that others had used them for their own political ends and a considerable number vowed that they would never allow this to happen again.

Interface violence
The topic of interface violence figured frequently in Community Dialogue seminars, both because it is an issue which impacts on Northern Ireland as a whole and because the wider situation impacts on what goes on at the interfaces. Also, some of our participants either lived in or worked with organisations involved in interfaces.

In 2004 there were 26 Government-built physical interfaces between Protestants and Catholics in Belfast alone. By 2004 most working class areas in Belfast were made up of one religion or the other. There were also many other geographical boundaries in Belfast and elsewhere separating the two communities.

At different times intercommunal violence at the interfaces intensified, often during the summer. This was due to a number of reasons: the pressure of outside events, e.g. the Drumcree parades in Portadown, outsiders who came into one or other of the interface areas and launched attacks, or youth violence. People were afraid for their personal security, the loss of their constitutional position and political identity and the future of their local communities. Demographic and economic change also led to the expansion of single identity areas. In Belfast there were more Catholics than Protestants looking for houses, while Protestants moved to other areas such as Larne, Carrickfergus and Newtownards. This left empty houses in Protestant areas in Belfast and the remaining Protestants wanted to block Catholics moving into them to avoid being outnumbered. This in turn was resented by Catholics looking for houses.

There was no evidence to suggest that people living within interface areas were more sectarian than the rest of the population. Nor did everyone in these areas assume that all those living on the other side of the divide were opposed to him or her. Despite this interface residents bore a disproportionate burden of the effects of sectarianism. The level of deaths during the Troubles rose the nearer an area was to an interface. A third of the politically motivated murders in Belfast between 1969 and 2001 occurred within 250 metres of an interface (Pete Shirlow, 'Who Fears to Speak: Fear, Mobility, and Ethno-sectarianism in the Two Ardoynes' in *The Global Review of Ethnopolitics*, Vol. 3, no. 1, September 2003). Secondly, each group often did not use shops, surgeries and other public services if they had to pass through the other community's territory to access these services. Many living in interface areas believed violence against them from the other side had increased since the ceasefires. Most had never had a conversation about political issues with people from the other side. They also experienced a 'chill' factor at work, so that the vast majority would not seek work where the other community was in the majority.

Many efforts were made to deal with the effects of interface violence. Among the most successful were mobile phone initiatives where leaders on each side could find out quickly the reality about incidents. However, these worked best when those involved knew each other well because they had engaged in a programme of joint activity and dialogue over many months. If this did not happen trust could break down because of misunderstandings about particular incidents and this sometimes made things worse.

There were several Government-led initiatives but these tended to be reactive and short-term. Clearly there was a need for long-term, joined-up strategies where statutory and voluntary agencies would work together with local people taking the lead, in developing interface areas socially, educationally and politically.

Interface violence also raised a crucial question: was it possible for people in Northern Ireland to live peacefully in segregated communities? The level of violence between 1998 and 2004 suggested the answer was No, unless relationships between the interface communities changed. But division has been a fact of life in the North of Ireland for over 100 years, so a second question arose: was it possible to manage the division better? Whatever the answers to these questions the level of interface violence will be affected not only by what goes on within interfaces, but also by what happens in their hinterland and in the wider political scene in Northern Ireland as a whole. (For an overview of the issue cf. Belfast Interface Project, *A Policy Agenda for the Interface*, 2004).

OTHER BLOCKS

POLICING
One of the most contentious issues in the peace process has been policing. This is not surprising as a major part of the armed conflict was between the IRA and the RUC since the British Government introduced the policy of 'Ulsterisation' in 1976, which put the RUC rather than the army in the front line of the fight against paramilitaries.

The Agreement on policing
Under the Agreement the consenting parties recognised that that there was an opportunity for a new beginning to policing and they hoped for a police service which would be representative of the make-up of the community as a whole and which, in a peaceful environment, would routinely be unarmed. The Agreement called for policing structures which were professional, effective and efficient, fair and impartial, free from partisan political control, accountable, representative and which conformed with human rights norms. All these were aspirations but a number of specific undertakings were also made:
   • The British Government agreed to appoint an independent Commission to make recommendations for future policing.
   • It agreed to set up a review of criminal justice.
   • It was also willing to devolve responsibility for policing and justice to the Assembly, if there was cross-party support for such a proposal.

These commitments were fulfilled once the British Government appointed the Patten Commission and implemented the review of the Criminal Justice system. Many assumed that the findings of the Patten Commission were part of the Agreement, but this was not the case. There had been no consensus about policing during the negotiations leading up to the Agreement. Because of this, decisions about it were shelved. The later negotiations in response to Patten were not part of the original Agreement. They were part of the continuing negotiations which followed it and which led in time to many smaller agreements.

Unionist concerns

Unionist concerns about policing focussed on concessions to Republicans. For many, one of their greatest difficulties was the change of the name from the RUC to PSNI. For them this represented a slight on the memory of those who had died in the RUC defending their country against terrorists. Now, in response to these same terrorists, the name of the organisation was changed. Secondly, enquiries into the past seemed to them to be one-sided: they focussed on what the security forces had done, not what paramilitaries had done.

Nationalist concerns

The nationalist approach to policing was divided. While both the SDLP and Sinn Féin had major problems with the RUC the former required fewer changes before they would take their place on the new Policing Board. The SDLP were unhappy with the Government's Policing Bill of May 2000 and submitted over 100 amendments to it. As a result they got a greater emphasis on community policing, ensured that the name 'RUC' could not be used on official documents, increased the power of the Board to get reports and set up inquiries, strengthened the role of the Ombudsman, and won the right of ex-paramilitaries to sit on District Policing Boards. They also got changes in human-rights legislation affecting the Police, the possible extension of the 50/50 Protestant and others/Catholic recruiting rule beyond ten years, easier secondment of members of the Garda from the Republic, and an assurance that up to 1200 of the new Part-Time Reserve would be Catholic. On the basis of these changes the SDLP endorsed the new Policing Board in November 2001.

Sinn Féin refused to recognise the RUC or the new PSNI as the legitimate police force of Northern Ireland even during the time they held ministries in the Executive up to the time of the fourth collapse in

October 2002. Many argued that there was a major inconsistency in being a member of a government while at the same time refusing to recognise the Police of the territory for which that government held responsibility. Republicans responded by saying it was vital to get the policing issue right before they joined any policing board. Secondly, they objected strongly to the British Government remaining in charge of policing. (The Government were willing to devolve policing to a Northern Ireland Executive when and if there was cross-community support for this).

They also argued that the recommendations of the Patten Report, which was for them a considerable compromise, had not been fulfilled. Patten had recommended an oath for all officers, but under the legislation only new officers were required to take it. There was no mechanism to expel those Sinn Féin regarded as human rights abusers. They wanted a timetable to change the religious balance of officers. They were unhappy with the balance of power between Chief Constable, the Policing Board and the Secretary of State, especially in relation to enquiries; they wanted the Special Branch abolished; and they regarded police raids on Sinn Féin offices in 2003 as being politically motivated. (In 2004 the Police Ombudsman found this was not the case).

Many Nationalists believed there was collusion between elements in the security forces and loyalist paramilitaries. Basing their argument in part on a BBC Panorama programme in June 2002 on Pat Finucane, a leading solicitor murdered in 1989, Sinn Féin alleged that:
- The man who supplied the information leading to his death was the British agent and UDA member Brian Nelson.
- The man who supplied the guns was William Stobie, a Special Branch agent and member of the UDA.
- The man who admitted pulling the trigger was a Special Branch agent and UDA member.
- In charge of all of these people was another Special Branch agent who was at the time a UDA commander.
- British Military Intelligence and RUC Special Branch knew exactly what was happening as the plot unfolded. Yet they did nothing to prevent it.

In response to nationalist concerns the British Government appointed Judge Cory to assess whether or not enquiries should be held into the cases of Pat Finucane, Billy Wright (a Loyalist leader murdered in the Maze prison), Robert Hamill, murdered by a crowd in Portadown in sight of two RUC men, and Rosemary Nelson, a solicitor who had acted on behalf of the Garvaghy Residents in Portadown. Cory recommended that public enquiries be held into all the cases. The Government agreed in principle, but by the Summer of 2004 had still failed to set up the Finucane enquiry.

How valid were nationalist concerns? The refusal of Sinn Féin to take their places on the Policing Board impacted on the level of nationalist confidence in the Police. It was obviously a difficult step for Republicans. As with other major steps in the past timing was critical. Republicans themselves were the best judges of when such a move might be made without a major split. The implications of the move were obvious: Tony Blair argued that 'the concept of Republicans on the policing board, of young Republicans becoming police officers, while maintaining an active paramilitary organisation, outside of the law, only needs to be stated to be seen as an absurdity. There can't be two police forces' (quoted by F. Millar, 'SF, UUP on verge of a massive move forward', *Irish Times*, 18 Oct 2003).

The issues raised by Sinn Féin were important but they were open to a variety of solutions. The structure of the relationship between the Board, the Chief Constable and the Secretary of State was about balancing police accountability with operational independence. There was no easy answer to this. It would have been wrong to have politicians tell Police how to do their day-to-day job because this would allow for political interference. Given this, it was always a balancing act to ensure real accountability of the Police. Because of this it was unlikely that this issue on its own would be an Agreement-breaking one.

Secondly, behind many of the disputes about policing lay disagreement about how to handle the past. As we point out in Chapter Three there are only a number of ways to do this and each has disadvantages. Enquiries into the past, for example, are unlikely to deliver much truth, they are likely to focus on abuses by the security forces and not by paramilitaries, and they are therefore likely to be used as a weapon for each side against the other. This issue is discussed more fully in Chapter Three.

Thirdly, the issue of devolving policing to the Executive was not one with which the British Government had a major problem, provided both Unionists and Nationalists agreed to it.

Within the PSNI the Patten proposals made an impact on morale, some of it negative. Large numbers reported sick. New health and safety standards influenced the extent to which officers would intervene in riot situations. The reduction in numbers meant that often there was no capacity to respond to less serious crimes: anecdotal evidence suggested that many people did not get a quick response from the Police when in need. There were also positive responses with many within the Police anxious to respond to the new context of a reduction in violence and to move on from the past by building relationships with loyalist and republican communities.

Policing, like so many other issues in Northern Ireland, often got buried under unionist or nationalist ideologies. Government decisions, perhaps inevitably in a divided society, were often made for political and not policing reasons. The reality was that the police service, either in its structures or practice, was never going to be perfect. Society seemed to be becoming more violent, drug wars raised complex issues, and police officers were asked to act on behalf of the public using minimum violence. Talk about policing sometimes sounded as if it referred to an idealised world. Reality was different: even with the best police service in the world it would not always be possible to clear bars at closing time through mediation alone.

Yet despite the complexity and the political divisions negotiations slowly and grindingly led to a measure of agreement. The SDLP, representing about 44% of the nationalist community, together with the main parties, joined the new Policing Board and many believed Sinn Féin would join sometime either in 2004 or shortly afterwards. That situation would have been unimaginable a few years previously.

There was one final irony in the policing issue. At the start of the negotiations Republicans had been opposed to a Northern Ireland Assembly on the grounds that they wanted a United Ireland, not a Northern Ireland with a parliament devolved from Westminster. Yet as the process developed they pushed hard to have a date set for policing to be devolved. That was an indication of the degree of change through which Republicans went in the course of the peace process. In so doing they were no doubt hoping that one of their nominees would be the Minister in charge of policing. Yet inevitably the proposal also opened the possibility of a UUP or DUP nominee. The last time this happened was during the old Stormont regime. The difference this time was that major government decisions could not be taken without the consent of both Unionists and Nationalists.

LACK OF DIALOGUE
As we have seen, segregation between Unionists and Nationalists

increased between 1998 and 2004. Partly as a consequence there was little dialogue between the two sides. At a political level, David Trimble of the UUP and Gerry Adams of Sinn Féin did not have face to face negotiations until 10 September 1998, several months after the Agreement. The DUP at the time of writing still avoided any direct negotiations. At the wider public level there was even less contact. In Community Dialogue meetings, and in those of other similar organisations, participants often spoke about contentious political issues for the first time with people from a different political community. In these circumstances it is little wonder that each side often seriously misinterpreted the intentions and actions of the other.

This lack of understanding was inevitable given the slow pace at which direct talks developed among the leaders, and even then the vast majority of members below the leadership level never engaged in dialogue with their opposite numbers. Given this, the role of intermediaries was of some importance in the early stages.

However, it is important to note that this segregation and general lack of dialogue did not block the process. It continued despite these disadvantages. This again illustrates the difference between Northern Ireland and some other conflict situations. When politicians from the main parties in Northern Ireland visited South Africa in 1996, Nelson Mandela had to meet Unionists and Nationalists separately because the unionist group would not sit down with Republicans. However, as the process in Northern Ireland developed this refusal to meet changed slowly. At the end of 2003, just before the election, David Trimble appeared on TV alone and in a most relaxed style with Gerry Adams. During the following year a mixed community group, hosting a delegation from the Middle East, were amazed that they had to organise separate buses for Israelis and Palestinians. So the process had moved from a stage of frozen relationships to one in which there was considerable warmth in some sections of the Community Sector and some leading politicians knew each other well, although negative attitudes still persisted in the community at large. This illustrates the importance of keeping the process alive, of allowing relationships between individuals to develop, and of giving the wider public time to get used to unpalatable changes. These on their own would not have led to change. The carrot of the possibility of exercising power in a devolved government, and the stick of facing direct rule from London with a strong in-put from Dublin, were important. So also was the reality that each side had a veto over the conditions for devolved government.

AMBIGUOUS LANGUAGE

Lee Ross of Stanford University (in the Community Dialogue-Stanford Center study) has argued that ambivalent language can be useful, but only if negotiators believe that the issue blocking them is likely to become less important in the future. If they believe that it will remain as important, or become more so in the future, then it is better to find precise language to deal with it in the short-term.

The outstanding issues before the Autumn of 2004 were 'guns and government', paramilitary activity and policing. The longer the peace process lasted and the more Sinn Féin gained through politics, the easier it became for Republicans to consider changing their stance on these, something which earlier in the process had been unthinkable for them.

It was obvious that the IRA would have to face decommissioning but a major carrot was held out to them with the prospect of stable political institutions in which Sinn Féin would be the leading nationalist party.

The second problem - paramilitary activity - was not an issue which would terminate political negotiations, provided that the IRA convinced Unionists that officially it would no longer be active.

The third issue - policing - was a deeply emotional issue because so much of the republican struggle had been against the Police. But policing is a complex topic. The key emotional hurdle Republicans faced was to take responsibility for it by joining the Policing Board. If they crossed that hurdle everything else would be secondary. It seemed likely that this would be one of the eventual outcomes of the Leeds Castle Talks in September 2004.

It therefore transpired that in the Northern Ireland peace process ambiguous language turned out for the most part to be a positive element in the process. This is an example of issues not becoming less important in themselves, but becoming more manageable in a changed context.

This outcome did not seem likely for much of the time during the peace process because ambivalent language was a key factor in Unionists gradually rejecting the Agreement. However, this dissatisfaction led to the emergence of the DUP as the leading unionist party. This meant that they would have far more power in any new devolved government. But in turn this was dependent on their coming to terms with Republicans. It was fortuitous that this happened at the very moment when Republicans were most likely to be open to further change both because of concessions they had already won and because they also were the leading party within their own community.

All the above comments apply to the *political* process. They suggest that at this level a deal was more rather than less likely. However, at a community level it was different. There the ambiguous language helped harden, not soften, attitudes. So also did segregation and the fact that such a small percentage of people took part in dialogue over contentious issues. The gap which had existed between the Assembly and the Community Sector on the ground, during the times when the Executive was up and running, was likely to continue. Disputed parades, which were always a symptom of the wider rifts in Northern Ireland, threatened at times to destabilise the process. As the wider conflict lost much of its emotional tension so also the parades issue gradually became a less dominating problem, in part because of the work by ex-paramilitaries to restrain people in local communities. While community problems were likely to continue, the prospect of a political agreement involving the two allegedly most extreme parties, the DUP and Sinn Féin, meant that a significant piece of the peace jigsaw - a devolved government - might soon be in place.

LACK OF CONFIDENCE

Confidence between the principals was at a low ebb from the very beginning of the peace process. The 1998 Agreement was reached without face-to-face meetings between the main protagonists. Unionists constantly took the view that the IRA would return to violence, Republicans that Unionists were bent on excluding them from government. Each did not trust the undertakings of the other.

At one level this was less important. The structural factors in the conflict meant that it was impossible for one side to overcome the other. Nor could there be devolved government in Northern Ireland without the consent of each. These however were negative safeguards. To make positive moves confidence was necessary. Unionists wanted reassurance that the war was over. The way they chose to obtain this was less than ideal. By focussing on decommissioning they allowed Republicans to wring more concessions from the process in return for each act of decommissioning. Secondly, decommissioning was always going to give only weak reassurance since rearmament was always possible if Republicans chose it. Unionists would have been better advised to listen to those who knew the republican movement and pointed to the huge significance of Republicans being willing to take their places in a government devolved from the Westminster Parliament.

From their point of view Republicans increasingly came to the view that there was no point in making further concessions: no matter what they did Unionists would simply demand more. In particular many came to believe that Unionists would always erect some road block to any stable political institutions which included Republicans.

At the same time the continued existence of the IRA undermined unionist confidence. In turn that impacted on what Republicans wanted to achieve for themselves because it led to four suspensions of the Assembly.

Yet despite this lack of confidence, which at times seemed so strong as to make any further progress impossible, the process continued to develop. The success of the DUP and Sinn Féin at the polls was undoubtedly important. So also was a point consistently stressed in this book, the passage of time with the peace process still alive: as time passed people got space to get used to unpalatable realities, and they also learned that some of their worst fears were unfounded.

UNIONIST ALIENATION

Many Unionists continually felt alienated by the process. As they saw it the British Government made one long list of concessions to Republicans. In part this was because Unionists had little knowledge of the cost Republicans paid for their concessions. Secondly, they had to come to terms with a new situation: instead of writing Republicans off as terrorists they had to deal with them in the political process. Thirdly, while they obviously gained from the Agreement by maintaining Northern Ireland as part of the UK that gain did not outweigh the pain of having to deal with those they saw as their arch-enemies.

CONCLUSION

As we saw at the beginning of this section Northern Ireland was politically stuck in 2004. It was not obvious how the peace process was going to move forward. Nonetheless there were major factors which made it likely that there would be a return to devolved government in the not too distant future. One was that the Agreement was not dead, as so many proclaimed. The institutions in Northern Ireland were an important part of the Agreement but still only a part. The relationship between the two Governments was another vital part and not only was that still in place but it had strengthened and deepened since the signing of the Agreement because that was in the interests of the Governments.

Secondly, the Executive existed, on and off, for a period of just over four years. During that time local politicians got a taste of what they could do in government. All the parties wanted a return to devolved government. They simply disagreed on the conditions necessary for this to happen.

Thirdly, Republicans constantly went further than they said they would. It was dangerous to assume that they could continue to do this, but a number of factors made it likely that they would do so. One was that the political success of Sinn Féin gave them an alternative to violence. The political path contradicted the use of violence and this became increasingly obvious: it was why the Executive collapsed so often. There was no enthusiasm among any significant section of Sinn Féin supporters for a return to violence. To do so would have destroyed Sinn Féin's political gains. In order to build its political base further the party needed to be involved in government. Further after the 9/11 attack in the US terrorism was an even more unpopular path in the West and there was less tolerance for ambiguity about it. For all these reasons Republicans were likely to do whatever was necessary to get back to devolved government, provided that this time they believed that the institutions would be stable, and that the rules gave them similar opportunities to those in the current Agreement. But it was clear that they would not accept any outcome which they saw as surrender. Since the DUP wanted devolved government, and knew, despite their rhetoric, that they could not have it without Sinn Féin, they were likely to come to an agreement in the long run.

In the post-Agreement situation the wider public, and not only the politicians and paramilitaries, were to play a major role. The issues which we have discussed in this section were hotly debated among and between Unionists and Nationalists. However, there was one issue which seemed to dominate for much of the post-Agreement period: how to deal with the past. This is the topic for the next section.

3

From Victimhood to Survival?

OPTIONS FOR DEALING WITH THE PAST

INTRODUCTION

As with other areas coming out of conflict, a major bone of contention in Northern Ireland has been how to deal with the past. This is not surprising. Killings are of real people with a web of family, relatives, friends and work colleagues. But beyond that killings were also often seen and meant to be seen as attacks on a whole community. So the community at large not only grieved for those killed, but also feared future killings. The outcome - inevitable in any violent conflict - was deep pain at both a personal and communal level.

The conflict was about many things. One of these was the legitimacy of the State. As a result there are different moral assessments of the past, varying from those which characterise it as a conflict between security forces doing their duty against criminals on behalf of a democratically appointed government, and those who see it as one in which an oppressed people went to war against an illegitimate government. Given these differences agreement about the past is unlikely. Our memory of the past not only deals with our pain. It also responds to our current needs, including those related to our present-day conflicts.

There is only a limited number of approaches to handling the past after inter-communal violence. All bring difficulties. Among them are:

- Legal justice.
- Reconciliation.
- Truth.
- Amnesia.
- A mixture of the above.
- Staying stuck in the past.

It is worth looking at some of the benefits and disadvantages of each. But it is also worth remembering that we cannot simply wish away the pain of the past. We have hurt each other too deeply for that to be possible. So talk of closure is nonsense. Also, there are many things we may want to happen about the past which are not possible. However, we can make things better or worse for ourselves in the future depending on which option we choose, and we will now look at five of these options.

LEGAL JUSTICE: THE SHYLOCK APPROACH?
Calling the legal approach the 'Shylock approach' may seem like giving it a bad name. However, the point about Shylock, in Shakespeare's play *The Merchant of Venice*, was that he used the law to achieve his ends and it backfired on him. Shylock had lent money to Antonio which had to be paid back by a certain date. If he failed to do so he had to pay a pound of his own flesh instead. Antonio invested his money in ships, all of which were lost at sea, so he was unable to pay back the loan. Shylock went to law and demanded his pound of flesh. In court Portia (who is also Antonio's lover) argued that he was entitled to a pound of flesh but only if he did not take one ounce of Antonio's blood because the agreement was to take only his flesh. This of course was impossible. In this case the law turned out to be the friend of the aggrieved Antonio.

In the aftermath of a major conflict legal justice can work - and then only partially - when people either accept the legitimacy of the State and therefore of the courts, or else when one side wins and can impose its view on the other. In Northern Ireland Republicans failed to remove the British Government, but the British Government also failed to win agreement about the State (although those who voted for the Agreement accepted that Northern Ireland would remain part of the UK until the majority North and South decided otherwise).

Applying legal justice to the past would mean prosecuting all those involved in what the State saw as a crime. This would be difficult because the length of time involved in many cases made it difficult to acquire evidence. Also the IRA destroyed a lot of evidence when they blew up the Forensic Laboratory in 1992.

If the Government had insisted on pursuing legal justice there would have been no Agreement, at least none involving paramilitaries because they would have had no incentive. (Some would see that as a good thing, but the price would have been the continuation of a much higher level of violence). Once the Agreement had been made, no matter what difficulties it ran into, the Government was going to put little effort into pursuing people for crimes committed during the

Troubles. To do so would have destabilised the situation and that would have been against its interests. One example is that of Joseph Magee who was given a life sentence in 2004 for the murder of Sgt Michael Newman in 1992. However, the early release scheme set up under the Agreement meant that he would serve only a few months.

The post-9/11 international context has made it more difficult to bring governments to account for human rights abuses committed in the past, because more attention is paid to national security and less to rights. (Changes to US and UK laws on detention are examples of this).

All this means that people who want prison sentences for those they believe are guilty of crimes committed between 1969 and 1998 are unlikely to be satisfied.

Civil actions may produce more results. In 2003 the Omagh Victims' Support Group served writs on five people suspected of involvement in the 1998 bombing, seeking £10 million damages. The following year, after a public appeal, the British Government announced that they would help to raise the balance needed to mount a legal case. If the Omagh Victims succeed it may open the way for other claims against individual paramilitaries. There are precedents elsewhere for this approach. In 2004 a Geneva-based Roma organisation won the right in court to sue IBM for allegedly helping the Nazi extermination of 600,000 Roma. If successful this could lead to a $12 billion suit. If international law develops - and progress was made in this with the genocide trials from the early 1990s - the issue of compensation may become more prominent. But how will large States respond? For example, what will happen if European States are asked to compensate African States for the terrible crimes of colonialism?

RECONCILIATION: THE SOFTLY-SOFTLY OR REALIST APPROACH?
Reconciliation means many different things to different people. For some it means simply that warring parties stop fighting and manage to work together. For some, among them many influenced by Christian theology, it means that victims forgive, perpetrators repent, the truth is told, justice is seen to be done, and everyone gets on together. For others it means pursuing criminals and locking them up. Still others say reconciliation can only be achieved when the truth is told, even if there is no justice, forgiving or repenting. Other views are a mixture of some or all of these elements.

In other cultures, for example in the Arab world, a victim may, as an act of nobility, decide to forego restitution. In Christian theology any element of reconciliation can be started by any party. So a victim may decide to forgive without the perpetrator repenting or a perpetrator may repent without being offered forgiveness by the victim. This is an important point because sometimes victims feel guilty that they are not reconciled with their enemies, when in fact all they can do is to forgive. It is up to the perpetrator to repent and if he or she does not there is nothing further the victim can do. Each side in a dispute is responsible only for their own actions, but clearly for there to be reconciliation movement by both is necessary. (Many Christians take a different view of the New Testament and believe that the victim is only required to forgive when the perpetrator has repented).

The 1998 Agreement allowed for the early release of prisoners without any requirement on them to admit wrong or to tell the truth. (Nor was there any obligation on individuals in the security forces who had abused human rights to admit wrong). There were different responses to this:

- Many thought this was the right thing to do because they believed that those who had fought on their side were justified in their violence.
- Others believed that those who used violence had been wrong, but so were individuals and/or groups within the security forces. Most of these were not punished, so why should paramilitaries be singled out? Some who hold this view reject the legitimacy of the security forces as a whole. Others accept their legitimacy but reject the actions of those who act outside the law.
- Some objected to calls for reconciliation. Given the early release of prisoners, they argued that such calls end up as calls on victims to forgive. Why, they ask, should victims be asked to make some move while perpetrators are not? This makes victims doubly burdened by the perpetrators' crimes.
- Some said it was morally wrong to release prisoners early because the Bible gives the State a duty to punish wrongdoers. Further, what faith can be put in law when murderers are released and tax evaders or drunken drivers have to serve their full sentence? (Others hold different interpretations of the Bible).

Those who emphasise the importance of reconciliation argue that without relationships and understanding developing between the political parties and communities the peace process will not be sustained. Unless the past is dealt with it will continue to impact negatively on the present. They point to the four suspensions of the Executive as evidence of this. They therefore see the need for some sort of Truth and Reconciliation process in Northern Ireland which will give space for relationships to be healed.

The contrary view is put by those who believe reconciliation between former enemies, while desirable, is either unnecessary or unobtainable. They believe talk of 'reconciliation' in political conflict makes no sense, any more than it would if discussing tax policies or class structures. (When did you last ask 'Are you reconciled with the tax man'? Or: 'Should the working classes forgive the middle classes for their economic exclusion?'). They believe reconciliation language confuses interpersonal or inter-group relationships with political systems, which are dominated by self-interest. 'Reconciliation' may be an ideal sought by individuals or Churches, but in this view it is not appropriate at the level of politics. The task of peace work is not reconciliation, but to help groups end violent conflict.

These two approaches are deeply divided on what needs to be done about the past. Nonetheless, the term 'reconciliation' is used by both. The term is also used frequently by funders in Northern Ireland: they often want their money spent in the cause of 'reconciliation', even though the projects they fund not only vary widely but may even be in tension with each other. The same funding organisation may support one project dealing with human rights abuses which aims to punish individuals for past wrongs, and also another project aiming to build relationships between opposing communities. Both are lumped under the heading of 'reconciliation', but there is a tension - often unexamined - between the two aims: locking people up often works against building good relationships.

It is clear from this discussion that as soon as someone uses the term 'reconciliation' in politics it is necessary to ask them what they are talking about. For this reason alone it seems preferable to use a different term.

If people take a New Testament approach and focus on forgiving, repenting, justice and truth they are arguably setting too high a goal for secular society. Organisations in society are not people: they are groups. There are serious philosophical, theological and practical difficulties in asking groups to apologise or forgive for the past.

Two basic questions need to be answered: what wrong was done by whom to whom? And, who benefits from a focus on reconciliation: the victims, the perpetrators, or wider society?

Historical wrongs are more difficult to handle. For example: should the Irish forgive the English for the Famine? Should the English apologise to the Irish for the wrongs done during the Famine? These raise at least the following further questions:

- Did the English historically wrong the Irish during the Famine? (Some historians dispute this).
- Is there some connection between the English who did wrong and the current British Government?
- Is there a connecton between the Irish who were wronged back then and Irish people today?
- Can these Irish people forgive on behalf of their ancestors?
- Can the British Government apologise (which implies the present Government is responsible for what was done), or regret the actions of a previous British Government (which implies that the present British Government is not responsible for what previous Governments have done)?

These questions raise the extent to which bodies like governments can take corporate responsibility and how far this idea should be extended. Corporate responsibility is a recognised concept in international law: present-day governments can be sued for what their predecessors did. But how far back should this apply?

Further, if the English apologised for the Famine and the Irish forgave them, would this improve relationships between the British and Irish States? If not, what would be the point of the apology and forgiveness?

Another example is that of apologies for violence during the Troubles. Should the IRA or Loyalists or the British security forces apologise for what they did? In all three cases most of those involved within each group seem to have thought what they were doing was morally just, so how can they apologise for it?

If we want to make peace it is certainly preferable to focus on wrongs our own group have done and to apologise for them rather than seeking apologies from others.

Whatever one's view, at the very least one can see from this discussion, which could be extended at length, that this issue is complex. Focussing on it may have the unintended result that we continue to have endless discussions about the past when the purpose should be to move away from this and focus on the present and the future. This is not to say organisations and governments should never forgive, apologise or make recompense. It is simply to highlight the problems involved, which are often ignored.

It is worth noting that we could get to a stage in which the past plays a less significant role in Northern Ireland politics without any group forgiving or repenting. And this is just as well because examples of groups doing either have been rare.

None of this is to play down the importance of forgiving, repenting, justice and truth. Nonetheless, these ideas work best with individuals and to a progressively lesser extent as we move from an interpersonal into a wider, larger and more complex political context.

Finally, one point where the ideal of reconciliation can work at both the individual and the wider political level is through the example of individual leaders. Nelson Mandela was able to forgive those at whose hands he suffered. As a political leader this capacity to forgive influenced the leadership he gave. As part of this he insisted that former members of the National Party, who had supported apartheid, had a future in the new South Africa. Doing so helped reduce racial tension in the country.

TRUTH: THE DETECTIVE APPROACH

Truth can be defined in different ways. For those who see it as part of reconciliation some form of Truth and Reconciliation Commission (TRC) is vital. For those who see it as an element of justice, enquiries into the past or legal processes are what matter most.

Truth and Reconciliation Commissions?

There have been many examples in recent years of Truth and Reconciliation Commissions as a way to deal with the past. The South African example is one of the best known.

The South African context was different from that of Northern Ireland. At the end of the conflict the anti-apartheid side won: there was a change of government. In Northern Ireland at the end of the conflict there was a stalemate. As a result the settlements in the two countries were different. In South Africa a perpetrator could be given amnesty only if he or she had committed a crime which was defined as political and if he or she was found by a court to be telling the full truth about the incident. If they fulfilled these conditions they got a complete amnesty, which included the right to retain their job, for example in the security forces.

Jeffrey Benzine is an example of the latter. He was a police officer who tortured people to extract information. (He put a wet bag over their head and choked them almost to the point of death). The Amnesty

Commission of the TRC found that his crime was political and that he had told the truth. This meant that he got a full amnesty and he kept his job as a police officer.

In Northern Ireland there was no amnesty: prisoners were released on license and remained subject to the same discrimination in civil society as other convicted ex-prisoners. They did not have to admit any crime. Nor were they required to tell the truth about they had done. If the South African process was about amnesty, the Northern Ireland approach was about amnesia or forgetting about the past. It involved a pragmatic drawing of a line in the sand and moving on for what was seen as a greater good.

In South Africa there was a Human Rights Violations Committee which formally heard testimony on behalf of the State from victims. There was also a Reparations Commission to which victims could apply. In Northern Ireland victims could apply for compensation to the courts - although those with convictions were normally excluded from this - and a Victims' Commission was set up after the Agreement which offered some financial assistance to victims' groups.

The South African Truth and Reconciliation Commission was intended to mark a transition period from the past to the future. There are different views about its success, but there was no similar formal process in Northern Ireland.

A TRC for Northern Ireland?
In Northern Ireland political prisoners have already been released. There are a number of outstanding issues such as the question of the 'on the runs' and whether or not political prisoners should be freed from the legal discrimination which operates against all former prisoners. Would the carrot of an offer to deal with these issues be so attractive to paramilitaries that their organisations would tell the full truth about past operations, including those, which even by their own standards were unacceptable?

Secondly, why would the British Government tell the truth? To do so would mean opening its files, including intelligence files. These would show the murky deeds committed by some members of the various security forces, with or without government approval. The embarrassment to politicians and political parties might well be great. There would be implications for the security of informers. What motive would the Government have for doing this?

Thirdly, any Irish Government intelligence cooperation with the British, and possible deals it made with paramilitaries, would also be exposed. Again, why would the Government tell the truth?

If there is to be a TRC we need to show how the different agencies can be persuaded to tell the truth. One view is that aspects of the past have leaked out and will continue to do so, but this will be mainly about security force, not paramilitary, activity. This has been largely due to whistle blowers. However, some paramilitary activity has also surfaced, for example, about the disappeared.

Others maintain that until we acknowledge the truth about the past we will not be able to move on. But this is to make an assumption which may or may not be true. The assumption is based on psychological theories of the individual about the need to deal with past traumas. Even with individuals it is not always best to face the past, because sometime individuals either do not have the capacity or in some cases the need to do this. All psychological theories concerning individual behaviour are difficult to prove and this is all the more true when applied to societies. Other theories suggest that our need to look at the past is deeply influenced by our current situation. In this view if we are more secure about our present situation we may be less inclined to look at the past. We should be cautious about all our theories because there can be no certainty about the best way to deal with the past.

A further assumption behind the idea of TRCs is that truth-telling helps victims. Many victims say they simply want to know what happened, and that they are not interested in punishment. But victims differ in their approach to the past as much as others. Some want justice, others amnesia. Some who now want truth may find, when they get it, that they also want justice. Some who discover the truth find that it does not help them.

Finally, some suggest what we need is not a Truth and Reconciliation Commission, but a Truth Commission, because including reconciliation - as they define the term - is too high a goal.

Inquiries into the past
Inquiries into the past may lead to an unequal outcome in that they are more likely to focus on abuses by the security forces than on those committed by paramilitaries. This is because successive British Governments always insisted they were fighting criminals within the framework of law (despite clear breaches of international human rights legislation, for example, with internment). They have therefore opened themselves to accountability before legal agencies. Further, human rights organisations take a greater interest in abuses by the

State than by non-state operatives. It is therefore likely there will be more Inquiries into incidents in which Republicans claim they were victimised by the security forces than into those where former security-force personnel suffered. Loyalists will also get fewer inquiries into incidents where they feel victimised, partly because to demand these means embarrassing the State with which they identify, however angry they may be at the way they were treated by that State.

This has already led to a situation where Unionists believe Republicans have received preferential treatment, and this issue has been raised frequently in Community Dialogue events. Many argue that if those linked to paramilitary groups are not punished and there are no enquiries into their activities, why should security force members not be treated in the same way? They also say it ill befits Republicans, given their own record, to complain that some former RUC officers, now in the PSNI, may have abused human rights.

Others respond by saying higher standards are expected from the State. Further, community groups, both republican and loyalist, would welcome learning the truth about State collusion. Republicans, however, do not recognise the legitimacy of the State and are therefore on weak ground in putting this argument. They also maintained that the context of the violence during the Troubles was one of war, yet today they judge the past actions of the State by the standards of normal democracy.

When many Unionists talk about the need for 'closure' this is one of the issues they have in mind: they do not want more enquiries into republican deaths at the hands of the security forces while the deaths of their own loved ones are ignored. One outcome of extended enquiries may be to increase the sense of unionist alienation. But Unionists in taking this stance are failing to demand a higher standard from the State than from paramilitaries. This raises questions about the essence of the unionist position that Northern Ireland was a democracy.

Inquiries also cost money. The Saville Inquiry by the start of 2004 had already spent over £125 million. There are cheaper ways to hold Inquiries, but in part this depends on the complexity of the issues involved.

The Chief Constable, Hugh Orde, pointed out in 2003 that there were 882 unsolved murders since 1969. Attempting to deal with these crimes took up a large proportion of police resources. He wanted an outcome which would avoid police time being taken up by cases that they could do little about and that would not lead to anyone going to jail because of the Agreement's commitment to early release. On the other hand, many individuals and families see Inquiries as vital to learn the truth about what happened to their loved ones and they believe that without this they will not be able to move on.

As with other ways of dealing with the past, enquiries may help with some things, but they will also create difficulties.

AMNESIA OR IGNORING THE PAST: THE OSTRICH APPROACH

Forgetting about the past is not an option. Northern Ireland society has been too deeply traumatised for that. But we could choose not to refer to it in public debate, or to give it less attention. Some argue for this on the basis that:

- Talking about the past is not going to achieve anything.
- It is counterproductive, either because it helps victims stay stuck in the past, or because it is used as a weapon by different groups to beat up others psychologically.
- Groups use the past to justify their own position which only increases division.
- Initiatives to deal with the past promise more than they can deliver, e.g. the suggestion that TRCs will deliver reconciliation.
- Amnesia was by default the route chosen by the 1998 Agreement: prisoners were released (although still subject to discrimination), no mention was made of enquiries into the past.
- The South of Ireland handled the legacy of the 1921-1923 civil war largely by silence: while political parties were formed on the basis of alignments forged during the war the atrocities committed were rarely spoken about. Some argue that this approach enabled the State to survive.

But amnesia has its own costs. Many will still want legal justice and if they cannot get it they will pursue enquiries. Others will say that reconciliation is the only way forward and therefore we need to look at the past and work towards forgiving, repenting, justice and truth. Many victims will still continue to cry out in pain. Like other approaches to dealing with the past, amnesia has both its costs and its benefits.

THE MOSAIC APPROACH

A mosaic is a multitude of different patterns coming together to make up one design. In terms of dealing with the past it means trying to take the best of all options and avoid the worst: this means that we should not do one particular thing but rather have a series of processes from which individuals choose what suits them at any given time. Many options are listed in the *Healing Through Remembering* report (Healing Through Remembering Project, June 2002). Among its recommendations are:

- A network to link together the diverse forms of commemoration.
- A process to gather the personal stories of people who wish to share them.
- An annual 'day of reflection'.
- A permanent living memorial museum, so 'that all organisations and institutions that have been engaged in the conflict...honestly and publicly acknowledge responsibility for past political violence due to their acts of omission and commission'.

The strength of the *Healing Through Remembering* report is that it suggests a variety of ways to commemorate the past. There will be difficulties with some of its suggestions, as there will be with all proposals to deal with the legacy of terrible and destructive violence.

Perhaps more important than arguments over how we commemorate the past are the motives we bring to any initiatives we take and the extent to which we are sensitive to the needs of others.

Whatever approach we adopt we should try to recognise both its limits as well as its potential benefits. The following issues are likely to come up.

RECURRING ISSUES

MEMORY AND RESENTMENT

Why do we remember the past?

- To score points against our enemies?
- To give vent to our anger and bitterness?
- To ensure that past atrocities will never happen again?
- To reinforce our identity?
- To communicate our pain and seek healing both for ourselves and others?
- Because we cannot forget past pain and because the pain, physical or mental, is still present?
- To honour our dead, to keep alive their memory and to provide a meaning for lives which were lost in violence?

Memory is crucial because the stories we tell to our children are influenced by it. That in turn influences the type of society future generations will be able to create. Also, if we can see nuances in the past it will help us accept apparently confusing situations today. One example of this is a British person of African descent who traced his genes to an African village and found he was descended from slave traders. Visiting the past can disturb our current view of ourselves.

What we choose to remember is also deeply influenced by the society we want to create. If, for example, we want to create a Northern Ireland in which Unionists and Republicans live a mostly separate existence then the stories we tell of the past are likely to be about the good things 'our' group did and the bad things the 'other' group did. If, however, we want to create a society with less polarisation we will want to understand why both groups acted as they did, and we will also want to explore the bad things our own group did.

While many victims may have limited choice over what they remember - the pain of the past can be like a pneumatic drill in the middle of their head - at a communal level we can make choices which influence to a degree what we remember.

One of these is to decide whether or not we want our communal lives defined by the past. How we respond to this choice will influence how we will see ourselves in ten, twenty and thirty years from now. So we can - to put some crude choices - remain a society still consumed by the past and define ourselves as the 'people of the Troubles', or we can be a society which has not forgotten the Troubles, one which still tries to understand why different people did what they did, but which is also interested in a vast range of other human issues such as: developing our role in the new Europe, building fair trade internationally, examining the impact of technology on the literary imaginations of young people, or trying to limit the damage to the environment of globalisation. We can decide to get a life beyond the Troubles - or not. We will decide our response to this issue by the communal stories we create for ourselves.

Erecting memorials to the dead of one group can cause offence to others because moral assessment of the past differs from group to group. Those offended overlook the humanity of the enemy and that suffering and pain affects all sides. Civil wars tend to be more bitter than conflicts between countries where sometimes people on each side are able to appreciate that the other side are fighting for their country just as they are doing, and in that way develop some respect for them. But in Northern Ireland many see everyone on the other side as simply

terrorists, colonial oppressors or dupes of colonialists. In that context
it is difficult to listen to, let alone understand, why they did what they
did. Others have more respect for their opponents while remaining
utterly opposed to what they did, and are therefore willing to try to
erect memorials in less offensive ways. An understanding of why
people did what they did in the past could grow if there was more
dialogue. That, in turn, while not leading to agreement, might lead to
respect, to a recognition that many groups need to remember the past,
and to finding ways both to make commemoration less militaristic and
less offensive to other groups.

It used to be the case that Nationalists harboured more resentment
about the past than Unionists. That became less true as the peace
process progressed. Many believed that Republicans, whom they saw
as terrorists, gained concessions through murder and mayhem. Some
would have been prepared to live with this if they believed the violence
was over, others would not have shared power with Republicans in any
circumstances. Unionists believed they have lost ground because of:
- The change in the name of the RUC which they saw as an insult
  to those who held the front line against terrorists.
- Changes in policing imposed by the Government which they saw
  as indicating that there had been something wrong with the
  security forces during the violence.
- The requirement of 50/50 Catholic-Protestant and others
  recruiting, which discriminated against Protestants.
- Changes in human rights which they saw as benefiting
  Nationalists disproportionately.
- What they saw as betrayal by the British Government in its
  failure to defend the Union, starting with Secretary of State
  Peter Brooke's 1990 statement that the British Government had
  no 'selfish, economic or strategic interest in Northern Ireland'
  and would accept the unification of Ireland by consent.
- Many of those Unionists who supported the Agreement in 1998
  felt in 2004 that they had been sold a pup: the IRA had not
  disbanded, paramilitary activity continued, and they were faced
  with other anti-Agreement Unionists telling them 'I told you so'.
- Loyalists believe they had been misled by their own politicians
  and were not treated on the same basis as Republicans because
  the latter had greater political influence.
- Most believed too much peace money went to nationalist areas.
- Unionist culture and identity was turned down like a dimmer
  switch.

The perception of unionist loss was shared by many who argued that the Government focussed on nationalist needs to the exclusion of those of Unionists and if this continued they believed the process would not survive.

Nationalists and Republicans responded to the above by arguing:
- That changes in policing were necessary because of the corruption of the security forces and militarisation of the Police.
- That the Patten Commission on policing was a compromise which many had difficulty accepting but that the British Government proposals fell well short of it.
- That 50/50 recruiting was necessary if the Police were to change from the former situation where less than 10% were Catholics.
- That the British Government should take a more neutral stance between the two communities instead of supporting the unionist case.
- That nationalist areas made economic and social progress because the people in them organised themselves.
- That Catholics were still twice as likely to be unemployed as Protestants (8.3% to 4.7% , Northern Ireland Statistics and Research Agency, *Labour Force Survey* 2001).

Resentment and bitterness are bad for us. They destroy us inside. They eat us up emotionally. They harm our health in very specific ways. Yet most of us, when faced with the terrible pain of losing a loved one through murder, would find it impossible not to feel bitterness.

The terrible reality is that victims face not only the injustice of losing their loved ones, but also an almighty battle to let go of bitterness or risk suffering further loss through destructive physical and mental pain.

This is also true at a communal level. One US commentator said in 2002 that he had never seen bitterness similar to that in Northern Ireland, not even in South Africa in 1993, when violence increased just before the peace agreement.

Others asked why bitterness was so deep when major violence, at least, had declined as a result of the ceasefires. Some said that it would be easier if there were secure political institutions in place. Others said that it did not feel to them as if the war was over, whatever about the ceasefires.

Communal resentment can be reduced by addressing the same questions individual victims face:
- What wrong has been done to you?

- By whom?
- What would it take to undo the wrong?
- If the wrong cannot be undone (e.g. in the case of a murder) how can you come to terms with this?
- What wrong has been done by you or by people in your community towards the community of the perpetrator?

Two examples: many Nationalists think the British Government stole their land. What land? Can they point to the field? If not, are they talking about land they lost as a people? But if they look into history they may find that land was taken from their ancestors, or they may find their ancestors were the people who took the land! If the land was taken from them what do they want done about it?

- An admission that it happened?
- The return of the land?
- Some other form of compensation?
- What about the rights of those who have worked the land over the past 400 years or so?

A second example: some Unionists still think all Catholics supported the IRA. It is not true, but these Unionists will only learn this if they take the time to talk to Catholics. But they will only do this if they want to do something about their bitterness.

VICTIMS/SURVIVORS

The individual level
Victims are mentioned in only three paragraphs of the Agreement. The Women's Coalition are credited with getting this section inserted. Many fear that victims/survivors will be forgotten. Many support groups for victims/survivors complain about a lack of resources and compare the response to them unfavourably with that towards other groups, e.g. ex-prisoners.

Community Dialogue is not a victims/survivors' support group. Nonetheless many of those who took part in our dialogues had suffered loss in the conflict. In our experience it seems to have been helpful for some to tell the story of their suffering when they felt they were being listened to respectfully. Others have chosen not to do this, either because they did not feel the need, or because they felt it would not help, or because they were unable to do so. Community Dialogue does not and would not pressurise people to talk about their pain. Further, while some may be helped by doing this, it does not seem helpful for others. Also, there is a danger that people who have suffered may not be helped to move on if they constantly re-tell their story. In this, as in so many other situations, it is a matter of judgment, of giving people space, of respecting difference, and of the time being right.

Some victims/survivors have moved to a situation where their lives are no longer dominated by the injustice that happened to them. Some have offered forgiveness to the perpetrators. Others have not. It is not up to any of us to pass judgment on what other people have or have not been able to do. It would also be wrong to put ideal goals before people in a way that increases the burden on them. That would be like saying everyone needs to climb Mount Everest, when the reality is that coming out their front door and not killing a perpetrator may be a far greater achievement for some.

At different times individual victims have told us they want one or more of the following:

- Recognition.
- An apology.
- Restitution.
- Punishment for the perpetrators.
- The truth.
- The past undone and their loved ones returned to them.
- A Place to be heard.

Most of these have one thing in common: they cannot be obtained at all, or else only to a very limited extent. Admitting and facing this is deeply painful. It is worth looking briefly at each of the above needs in turn.

- *Recognition:* this is a short word that refers to many things. One of these is a public statement that the killing of the victim was morally and legally wrong. For many victims this is very important. A second is a statement that the death of the victim is part of a wider struggle for good and against evil, and that there was therefore some meaning in the person's death. Remembrance Day ceremonies try to meet this need. So people who have lost loved ones in British wars feel through these ceremonies that the State values the sacrifice they and their loved ones made, that it was part of a struggle for democracy, or patriotism, or whatever value was stressed by the Government in the war. Their pain is recognised and valued. For the most part this experience is unlikely to be available to Northern

Ireland victims, except within the context of their own groups. This is because of disagreement about the State. The British Government will give a measure of recognition to security-force loss. Awarding the George Cross to the RUC was an example, but it was done in the context where the name of the police force and other significant changes were being made. For many victims these changes undermined any sense that their loss was being recognised. For republican victims the issue of recognition by the British State is obviously less likely, and not something most Republicans would be seeking.

- *Apology*: this depends on the perpetrating individual or organisation. Some individuals have repented of killings and made this known to victims. Many have not: they see the killing as justified in the context of 'war' or of 'the struggle against terrorism'. Some regret the pain caused, but see it as having been necessary in the context. Organisations are far less likely to apologise, except for incidents which they see as against their public beliefs. So Gerry Adams has expressed regret for some republican atrocities such as the Enniskillen and Shankill bombs, but not for the IRA campaign as a whole. The Government have for the most part defended actions by security-force personnel, or else made out-of-court settlements with confidentiality clauses, but Tony Blair has expressed regret for Bloody Sunday.
- *Restitution:* this is generally an issue addressed to governments. Some response has and will be made. But many complain that the amount they receive is pitiable and an insult given the terrible wrong committed. However, governments are always going to limit payments for several reasons: demands on resources, fear of precedents - payment to one victim means others can demand the same - and bureaucratic systems, like governments, will generally calculate levels of restitution against things like the dead person's potential earnings, etc., which many find deeply humiliating.
- *Legal punishment:* anyone convicted of crimes connected with the Troubles committed between 1969 and 10 Apr 1998 under the terms of the Agreement will get early release. These will still face the legal punishment of being subject to the same discrimination as other prisoners, but they will not face punishment beyond this. Others, both security forces and paramilitary members who were never convicted, will not face

any legal punishment.
- *Truth:* we have discussed above the difficulties with Truth Commissions. In the Northern Ireland context it seems likely that most victims will not learn a great deal more of the truth.
- *The past undone:* this is not possible.
- *A place to be heard:* this is one need which is achievable. It may be that a voluntary Truth Commission could meet this need. This would mean making a space where both victims and perpetrators who wanted to tell their stories could do so. It might also mean information from particular perpetrators being given to the relatives of their victims if both sides wanted this. However, such a process would need to be thought through carefully. What psychological services will be available for people who feel particularly traumatised by the process? Will the process be in private? If so, how will the power of a perpetrator with information be balanced against the powerlessness of a victim/survivor with none? If the process is in public, what protection will there be against people making false accusations?

The communal/political level

It is one thing to respond to victims/survivors at the individual level. It is a different matter to respond at a political level. At an individual level people, as much as possible, should be given whatever support they need, especially in training, counselling and financial support for groups working with victim/survivors. The Government needs to face the reality that the legacy of conflict is going to be with us for a long time. If they are going to respond to this seriously that means putting significant extra resources on a long-term basis into counselling and other psychological-support initiatives.

Secondly, politicians and civil servants dealing with victims' groups need specific training. Victims' groups complain that the process of getting limited compensation can add to their trauma. Some believe they are made to 'feel like beggars' (Wave Trauma Centre submission to Human Rights Commission, December 2001). Victims find the process involved in calculating the amount of compensation a cold process when placed against their experience of loss. Government departments have to show how they arrived at their figures and this exercise will always be experienced as cold and bureaucratic to others. It may help to work with victims' organisations to explain how they arrived at their figures rather than with individuals directly. Clearly, then, staff dealing with victims need specific training.

Thirdly, the Government should give support to a variety of initiatives - some of which are outlined in the *Healing Through Remembrance* report. The variety is important. Whatever one's views on the benefits of an initiative such as a Truth and Reconciliation Commission, a variety of initiatives will make a wider impact than a few. State efforts at recognition, compensation, and truth telling, if performed sensitively and if done in conjunction with victims' groups can make a positive difference for many individuals.

While State institutions need to recognise the trauma of victims/survivors, they also need to guard against setting up systems which will encourage people to stay stuck as victims. The State has a role in contributing to the public language we use about the past. So it is important to stress that the past cannot be undone, that people who did bad things can change, that we differ in our moral assessments of the past but we still have to live in the same country, that victims need to be respected, listened to, and given some measure of compensation, and that, as we have seen, there are no simple or easy answers to how we handle the past.

It may be a good thing at the right time and in the right context to ask victims' groups (as distinct from individual victims):

- What is it that you really want?
- Who can give this to you?
- Who cannot give this to you?
- What pressure or encouragement can you bring to bear on them to get what you want?
- How likely are you to persuade those who have the power to do so to give you what you want?
- In trying to persuade them to give you what you want, to what extent are you putting control over your future happiness in their hands?
- Given that you may well not get what you want, how can you move forward?

'Innocent' victims

Some Protestant groups have defined themselves as 'innocent' victims. They do so on the basis that their loved ones were killed defending the State against unjust aggressors, or doing legitimate work for the security forces. They share with many paramilitaries one similarity: they are convinced of the rightness of their cause, and this illustrates yet again our inability to agree on a moral assessment of the past. However, where Republicans are willing to dialogue with 'innocent' victims, many of those who define themselves as 'innocent' victims are not willing to reciprocate. 'Innocent' victims may lose out as a result. They will learn nothing about those who killed their loved ones, their motives, the situation they were in when they carried out the killing, the tensions internal to their organisations, and their future intentions.

Differing approaches to victimhood.
When the Jewish survivors of the Holocaust arrived in Israel after World War II they did not talk about their experiences. They were too traumatised and it was difficult to communicate the horror of concentration camps to others who had not experienced them. (The SS told Jews in Auschwitz that even if one of them survived no one would believe their story). Further, the new State of Israel did not value victims. Instead it valued fighting to survive. The new State was going to ensure that Jews could never again be massacred because they were going to build a State with strong defences. Victimhood sat uneasily with this project.

Other groups practised a similar form of public amnesia. In France few talked about those who collaborated with the pro-German Vichy Government during the Nazi occupation. Nor was there much discussion of those who cooperated with the Nazis to transport Jews to the camps. (The French trains for the death camps always left on time). Instead the Government emphasised the importance of all French people pulling together as citizens of the new France.

From about the 1960s this began to change. Younger Jews in Israel began to ask their parents what happened in the war. The Israeli State began to support efforts to commemorate the Holocaust. Over the years this developed into a vast effort supported by Jews and many non-Jews world wide. Many Israeli school children were brought on tours of Auschwitz and other camps. One writer sees these tours as parallel to Christian pilgrimages in Jerusalem, walking the way of the Cross: the students marched along the railway tracks in Auschwitz-Birkenau like Christians on the Via Dolorosa (Tom Segev, *The Seventh Million: The Israelis and the Holocaust*, Hill and Wang, 1993, p. 495). They brought books of prayers, poems, and psalms, which they recited in front of the ruined gas chambers. They played cassette tapes of music composed by a Holocaust survivor named Yehuda Poliker. And at one of the camps, a candle was lit in the crematorium, where the students knelt in prayer. There is a message in these visits: if the State of Israel had existed before Hitler there would have been no Holocaust.

Only in Israel can Jews be secure and free.

The Jewish Holocaust memorials have encouraged others who experienced oppression to look for similar recognition. The concept of victimhood also haunts Hindu nationalists, Armenians, African-Americans, American Indians, Japanese-Americans and homosexuals (Ian Buruma: 'The joys and perils of victimhood', *New York Review of Books*, Vol 46, No 6, April 8, 1999).

As with other issues concerning the past there is both good and bad sides to commemorating oppression. The good side is that we learn about history. We see what happened to our ancestors. We find out where we have come from. But it is arguably harmful to create an identity for ourselves focussed on our victimhood, because if we do so we remain victims, we do not move to becoming survivors. A South African trauma counsellor remarked once: 'I do not deal with victims. The victims are all dead. I deal with survivors'. It sounds harsh, but this counsellor was naming the task facing all victims: to move, however slowly, to becoming survivors, to reach a place where they do not deny what has happened to them, but where their lives are no longer defined by this.

Secondly, if we focus to too great an extent on our historical victimhood we face the danger of losing sight both of the suffering of other groups and also the extent to which our own group has caused it. Further, communal victimhood can feed the desire for revenge.

Most victims naturally go through a period of intense anger. Some are helped by getting an opportunity to vent this. Others are not. But all then face a challenge: what are they going to do about what has happened to them? Are they going to make this the centre of their lives until they die? Or will they slowly move to a stage where their lives are no longer dominated by it?

The difficulty faced by the State is to find a language about the past that can recognise the suffering of victims and respect those who have died - from whatever quarter - since they are all human beings, and at the same time encourage people to continue on the long, painful journey from victimhood to survival. Republicans have no difficulty in recognising the relatives of security-force members who lost their lives as victims, but some Unionists have a problem recognising republican relatives as victims because they see those who died as terrorists. The Government will be blamed by them if they treat all victims the same, but they will be criticised by Republicans if they insist on a hierarchy of victims.

Perpetrators

The 'bad guys'?
Given the fact that we disagree in Northern Ireland in our moral assessment of the past, we are going to argue about which individuals and groups were perpetrators. Because of this some people say we should never talk about 'perpetrators' because one person's terrorist is another's freedom fighter.

One approach is to ask how much freedom people have and how much their freedom is reduced by their context. Many who took part in the conflict say that what they did was right at the time. Others admit they acted wrongly, but in the context they lacked the freedom to choose, or were too young to make a choice, or were led astray by politicians. Others speak of the past as if there were no human beings involved: 'Bad things happened', or 'There was a war on', as if this absolves participants from all blame.

On the other hand, many argue that those who did wrong should take responsibility for what they did. They point out that not everyone who suffered terrible things, or came from a difficult background, killed people. Those who did are morally responsible.

It is easy to see why we are never going to get agreement on this issue. However, if we take the view that the context was so dominant that people had no freedom over what they did, then this means that nearly 3500 people were killed by what seems to be some form of accident. On the other hand, playing down the role of the context means ignoring the pressure there is on people to act violently. If that pressure did not exist far fewer human beings would have gone to war throughout history. And all wars involve terrible acts.

Perpetrators as victims?
Some ex-combatants and members of the security forces now argue that they are also victims because of the context they found themselves in. We are not unique in this. Jeffrey Benzine, the South African policeman mentioned above who got amnesty from the TRC, claimed he too was a victim. At the Truth Commission he engaged in dialogue with one of his victims, Tony Yengeni. The quotes which follow are from the transcript of the TRC hearing, 14 July 1997.

Benzine said he had to have the windows of his house barricaded. Every night a wet blanket had to be put in the bath which his children could get if the house was attacked by hand grenades. He suffered from his nerves, and his marriage nearly failed. 'Yes, Mr Yengeni', he said,

'I did terrible things, I did terrible things to members of the ANC, but as God is my witness, believe me, I have also suffered. I may not call myself a victim of Apartheid, but yes Sir, I also have been a victim'.

He said his motive was to get information from terrorists:

> 'Maybe I was too patriotic, too naïve or anything else that you would want to call it. But I think even you and the rest of your people sitting there, would admit that I was the person that rightly or wrongly could glean information from you and your members'

This led Tony Yengeni to ask a question which many victims ask:

> 'What kind of man uses a method like this one of the wet bag on people, on other human beings, repeatedly, and listening to those moans and cries and groans and taking each of those people very near to their deaths, what kind of man are you? What kind of man is that, that can do that kind of thing, what kind of human being is that Mr Benzine?

> 'I want to understand really why, what happened? I am not talking now about the politics or your family, I am talking about the man behind the wet bag. When you do those things, what happens to you as a human being? What goes through your head, your mind? You know, what effect does that torture activity have on you as a human being?'

Benzine replied that he had often asked that question himself and that he had gone to psychiatrists to get himself evaluated in order to find an answer to the question.

> 'There was a stage when this whole scene was going on, that I thought I was losing my mind. I have subsequently been, and I am now still, under treatment, where I have to take tablets on a regular basis'.

He said he wanted to protect White privilege, and also that he had never abused prisoners once he had got the information he needed. Further, that the torture was necessary in order to extract information about weapons and in that way to save lives. His sole objective was to get hold of weapons which would be used by freedom fighters against the public at large. He argued that, partly as a result of his actions, there was only one death in Capetown from pure terrorism. He also argued that he was simply being patriotic to his country, just as ANC members were. At the time he believed that what he was doing was right. He also believed that he was used by the Security Branch because of his commitment to his beliefs.

Yengeni was not initially supportive of Benzine's amnesty application:

> 'I think that when you spoke this morning, you indicated that you have reconciled with us and we have reconciled with you...but before I and my colleagues can express ourselves on supporting or not supporting your application for amnesty, we should be and must be convinced that you are speaking the truth...and by that you want the country to know what exactly happened. And until then, it is going to be very difficult for me and my colleagues to express ourselves on whether we support the application or not. We are prepared to support the amnesty application only on the basis of full disclosure and I am not sure that at this stage, we are ready, or that I am ready to say that you have made a full disclosure'.

This dialogue highlights a distinction which needs to be made between the ways in which perpetrators and non-perpetrators are victims. Sometimes the statement is made that we are all guilty. This emphasises that everyone is likely in some way, either by commission or omission, to have contributed to a context which made the Troubles more likely. But there is a difference between social guilt and the individual responsibility a person may have for killing someone wrongly, or encouraging others to do so, or being sectarian, however much that responsibility may be reduced by circumstances, such as age and context.

Secondly, it makes no sense to see a victim and a perpetrator as victims of the same incident. The person who killed someone wrongly was a perpetrator. The person whose loved one was killed was a victim. In the above example Benzine was a perpetrator, Yengeni a victim. Perpetrators themselves are damaged psychologically and morally by their crimes. Some suffer terrible physical damage, for example, those who have been injured by bombs they were planting. Some have described this pain very movingly. But to use the same term for them as for their victims is wrong. Of course it may be that the perpetrator is a victim in relation to other incidents and then the term 'victim' is appropriate, but only in relation to those other incidents.

Just as victims are faced with the journey of moving on to survival, so also perpetrators are called to move forward to a stage where they do not define themselves only as perpetrators. The past need not and should not define our future. Just as victims need to be able to move on, so too do perpetrators. For them, as for victims, counselling and other services may be necessary. They need programmes to integrate them into society. Of course many who are seen as perpetrators by others do not see themselves in that light because they regard what they did in the past as justified.

Forgiveness from a victim may or may not be available to a perpetrator (and it may or may not be appropriate to ask for it, as seeking it may put a greater burden on the victim), but even without forgiveness a perpetrator may still come to terms with the past. That may involve repentance, or it may involve recognising or at least regretting what was done in the past and committing oneself to working for a better society in the future. There is a continuing need for support groups for ex-combatants so that they learn to cope with what they have done.

The treatment of convicted paramilitaries

Early release of prisoners was a central demand of Republicans and Loyalists and undoubtedly helped the doves within the movement persuade others to accept a cessation of violence. Early release was also the most difficult aspect of the Agreement for Unionists. For some this was a religious problem: it meant the State was not fulfilling its God-given duty to pursue justice. For others it meant that what they saw as justice was not administered to make up for the wrong committed. This undermined their belief in the capacity of the State to deliver justice. However, it is difficult to see how there could have been an Agreement without early release. A precedent existed - all prisoners were released in 1961 within a year of the end of the 1956 border campaign - and given that the IRA had not been militarily defeated it is hard to see how Republicans would have accepted any settlement in the absence of early release.

Ex-combatants with convictions suffer from the same discriminations as other ex-prisoners. Among these are:
  • Difficulties getting mortgages and insurance cover.
  • Job discrimination because of their criminal record, e.g. they are ineligible for employment in the Civil Service.

They are blocked from:
  • Adopting or fostering children.

- Standing for election for five years after release.
- Membership of management committees of associations which provide services for young people.
- Getting taxi licenses for three years after release.
- If convicted under special powers legislation they are ineligible for compensation if they or their property is damaged in a sectarian incident.

Republicans and Loyalists argue that their ex-prisoners should not suffer these discriminations because they were political prisoners. Others take exactly the opposite view because they see them as criminals. Again this argument shows our inability to agree about our moral assessment of the past. But as with other aspects of the past there will be a cost involved no matter what view we take: if the wishes of ex-combatants are granted many, especially Unionists, will feel more alienated. If not, many ex-combatants will feel alienated. One of the likely costs of continued legal discrimination against ex-combatants is that it will be more difficult for them to reintegrate into society. If this happens will more of them revert to crime?

If everyone agreed to describe the conflict as a 'war' some of these problems would be overcome. Ex-combatants could be seen as POWs and this would remove them from any legal discrimination. The problem, of course, is that while Republicans want to characterise the struggle as a 'war', Unionists want to criminalize combatants, and on that issue there is likely to be no agreement.

This issue comes into play with particular force on the question of whether or not ex-combatants can join the Police, or with the possibility of an ex-paramilitary as Minister for Justice in charge of devolved policing. For some this is the ultimate nightmare. For others, it is a final sign that ex-combatants have become democrats.

At the bottom of this issue lies a question: do we want to punish those whom we blame for the Troubles? If we do, how will this affect political stability?

RECOMMENDATIONS
Given the different approaches to handling the past it will be difficult in the extreme to get a measure of agreement about it. Community Dialogue is made up of people from different political viewpoints. What follows then are personal views, since the organisation as a whole has no position on these issues.

It is important to distinguish different levels and to recognise that each needs to be treated differently at individual level, the macropolitical level and the micro-political level

At the individual level victims are forced to work out their own response whether they like it or not. They should be given much greater resources for counselling, training and other needs. It is up to themselves as individuals when and how much they want to move towards letting go and/or forgiving (which in the Christian view goes beyond letting-go). Churches can and should offer pastoral support. Above all they should help victims avoid inappropriate guilt over, for example, not being able to move to the heights of Christian forgiving.

Ex-prisoners are punished by discriminatory laws. These should be removed, unless there are clear reasons why some should be kept in place for specific cases. Why should any prisoner who has served his or her time be subject to further punishment not prescribed by the court when sentencing?

Again, as with victims, it is up to those who believe they have done wrong to decide how far they want to go in making public apologies. It would be nice if we were able to agree on a common moral viewpoint about the past but that is unlikely.

A Truth Commission?

A Truth Commission on the lines of South Africa will not work because our situation, unlike theirs, ended in a stalemate. There will be neither sufficient carrots nor sticks to persuade organisations to tell the truth. There is merit, however, in a voluntary commission, but its limits need to be recognised in advance so that it is not sold as something able to achieve impossible goals.

First it should be genuinely voluntary: no one can or should be compelled to appear. Why? Because if people are not willing to appear voluntarily they are unlikely to tell the truth. Compelling witnesses and giving the Commission powers to seize documents might elicit some degree of truth from State agencies, but it would not work with paramilitaries. A Commission focussed on only one party to the conflict will make it more rather than less difficult to focus on the future.

The purpose of the Commission should be to give space for victims and perpetrators who want to tell their story. Some of it will have to be in private. If information which is not already in the public domain were published it could be libellous. Individuals are entitled to protect their reputation. If one wanted to argue that the libel laws should be changed, the principle of protecting the innocent from libel would still stand. The only way around this would be to agree on judicial process which allowed public allegations to be made. This in turn would require a serious investigative branch of the Commission. That would mean that costs would soar and it would still be unlikely that much more truth could be obtained than currently exists.

As with all Truth Commissions we need to ask what happens when a person has told their story? Will they be offered on-going counselling? If not there is the danger that the Commission invites them to relive their trauma without further support and this could make their situation worse. Clearly, with these constraints, such a commission would be a very limited body. That is why it would be important not to raise false hopes in advance of it. Finally, if both particular victims and perpetrators wished, the information they give to the Commission could be shared.

Inquiries into the past
Three Inquiries were set up in 2004 and a fourth promised. As we have seen above these will focus on security force and not paramilitary abuses which will be seen, with some reason, as unfair by Unionists. They will almost certainly confirm a degree of collusion between the security forces and loyalist paramilitaries. They are likely to cost a lot and to unearth little new information. Only a few cases will be investigated. However, if they confirm collusion that will be a benefit: it will give greater authority to something which was merely a widespread belief. However, that should be the end of inquiries. They will not add anything positive in the future.

Moralism
There is a difference between a moral assessment of the past and moralism. The latter has been challenged in the Gospels: 'Why then do you look at the speck in your brother's or sister's eye, and pay no attention to the log in your own' (Mt 7:3 TEV). While other groups have certainly been wrong in what they have done, the same is also true of people in our group. To recognise this might help develop a degree of humility. That in turn might lead to more openness in dialogue which itself could lead to understanding.

Self-righteousness about the past is probably the biggest block to leaving the past behind. As one speaker at a Community Dialogue event said:

> 'I knew they were utterly wrong in what they did. But I did not realise that there might also have been some wrong on my side. I was only able to move towards this when I had listened to the stories of pain suffered by people in other groups'.

Those whom we believe have done wrong in the past are more likely to listen to us if we are willing to admit that our own group are not without fault.

It is on the micro-political level that much can be done. Through dialogue and teaching seminars both victims and ex-combatants can learn more about both their own and the other community. Secondly, they can learn more about other conflicts and realise that there are some similar dynamics elsewhere. Above all they may come to realise that the shocking pain we have inflicted on each other unfortunately does not make us unique: the history of the 20th century shows men and women very much like ourselves killing each other by the million. Learning that lesson may give us greater motivation to get away from simply blaming each other and to concentrate on building up structures, knowledge and training for the future, which will make the conflicts of the past, if not impossible, at least less likely. Most of our energies should be directed towards finding ways to learn this lesson.

It is at the micro-political level in community groups throughout Northern Ireland that people can tell their stories informally, without many of the legal binds which arise in more formal settings. Community groups can also give on-going support, unlike most Truth Commissions.

CONCLUSION

In Northern Ireland we have had over 30 years of killing. Over 3500 are dead, tens of thousands physically wounded, and who knows how many traumatised by the loss of loved ones. The cost of conflict is high. We cannot wave a magic wand over this pain and make it disappear. That is why talk of closure is so offensive. But we can make it easier or more difficult, for ourselves and others, to move on to a less destructive future. Using the past as a stick to beat our opponents will help to prolong bitterness. So also will using it to console our own group while ignoring the impact of our actions on others. Without the knowledge that comes from dialogue we cannot know the impact our words and actions might have on our children and others we influence. Much of our communal response to the past may emerge from throw-away comments made in front of our children while watching television. All of the issues relating to the past - Truth Commissions, inquiries, memorials, moral assessments, etc - are complex. But we can only realise how complex they are if we examine these issues together with others. As one woman who lost her son said: 'When the ceasefires came they told us we had to forgive. Now we realise that there is layer upon layer of complexity'.

4

Beyond the Stalemate?

THREE SCENARIOS

INTRODUCTION
There are two broad political directions we can take in Northern Ireland in the years ahead: one in which we overcome our divisions - gradually - and build a new political entity to which all are committed, irrespective of our wider, short or long-term aspirations; a second in which we continue to oppose each other, remain separate and cooperate only to the minimum level necessary to divide up Northern Ireland's wealth and/or external subsidies.

This section looks at each of these posibilities. Between them they raise three scenarios: an agreed Northern Ireland, a divided Northern Ireland and a United Ireland. It is worth looking both at the likely consequences of each of these and how likely each of them is to come about. This section also looks at some external factors which will make a major impact on our situation whether we like it or not.

SCENARIO ONE: AN AGREED NORTHERN IRELAND

To suggest that Unionists, Nationalists and others in Northern Ireland could agree about anything may seem highly optimistic, but in fact we are already agreed on much. However, for us to be united in a commitment to the political future of Northern Ireland, a number of things would be necessary.

Commitment to the people of Northern Ireland
Under the Agreement Ministers are required to take an oath promising to serve all the people of Northern Ireland equally. What does this mean? Does it mean Unionists must encourage Nationalists' political ideology or vice versa? Obviously not. It certainly means protecting Unionists and Nationalists from discrimination and from

lack of respect for their identity and culture. What are the implications of this if part of their identity means seeking a United Ireland or, alternatively, retaining the link with the UK? Can we really say we respect the identity of another if we actively seek to undermine something central to that identity? On the other hand, how can Unionists and Nationalists be expected to respect each other's identity if doing so requires giving up what is central to their own identity?

There are no easy answers to these questions but it would help if people focussed also on why they want the goals they seek. What is it about being part of the UK that matters most to Unionists? Why? What is it that matters most to Nationalists about being part of a United Ireland? Why? The answers to these questions will often throw up issues which are easier to deal with. For example, Unionists may say they value being part of the Commonwealth, or of the varied nationalisms in the UK, or of a State which still has influence on the world stage. Nationalists may say they see a United Ireland as the only long-term guarantee that they will not be treated as second-class citizens, or that they will feel at home in a place where the symbols of being Irish are accepted without conflict. All these are only some possibilities of what lies behind the desire to remain part of the UK or to join a United Ireland, but each of them is a potentially useful issue to discuss. Each reveals a need which could be met in a variety of constitutional systems. Unionists and Nationalists might not find agreement on their long-term constitutional goals, but they might well find agreement on the values which lie behind those goals, and in the end they may find that these are more important to them.

Acceptance of the territory of Northern Ireland
Unionists and Nationalists being united in a commitment to Northern Ireland presupposes a commitment to the territory of Northern Ireland, even if Northern Ireland becomes part of a United Ireland, or if any other constitutional form emerges.

The history of the eighty-four years since its foundation has given the people of Northern Ireland an experience different from that of people in Britain or the South. Customs and structures have evolved. The Agreement recognised at a formal political level the reality of unionist and nationalist political blocs. These are unlikely to simply disappear in any new dispensation. Unionists oppose a United Ireland in part because they fear discrimination. If they were assured that in any future Ireland they would retain the same protections which they currently enjoy under the Agreement, their fears might be reduced (although they would still want to remain part of the UK because of their British identity). This could only happen if Northern Ireland remained a political entity. In 2004 Sinn Féin was the sole party which wanted a unitary state. Changing this position to allow the continuation of Northern Ireland as a political entity would not compromise the long-term aim of Sinn Féin to achieve a United Ireland, since Northern Ireland could theoretically operate within a United Ireland, just as it currently does within the UK.

Similarly, if Nationalists really believed that they would be treated equally within Northern Ireland, and if they were also exposed to some of the difficulties involved in any move towards a United Ireland, more of them might be open to committing themselves to the people and territory of Northern Ireland.

In either case, however, in the absence of joint sovereignty, one side or the other will have to make the greater compromise in expressing their identity: if Northern Ireland stays in the UK, Irish political symbols on some occasions will play second fiddle to British symbols, and *vice versa* if Northern Ireland becomes part of a United Ireland. If a strong commitment to Northern Ireland emerged it could develop its own identity symbols. If these embodied significant respect for both British and Irish traditions, then the fact that on some occasions one or other of these were given priority would be less of a problem. Both Unionists and Nationalists could remain separate groups but in a context where each felt respected by the other.

Legitimacy of the British Government
Under the principle of consent in the 1998 Agreement there will be no change in the constitutional status of Northern Ireland without the consent of the majority North and South. The people of Ireland approved the Agreement in referenda, North and South. From a nationalist point of view the Agreement is the will of the people of Ireland. The corollary of this is that the legitimate Government of Northern Ireland for the time being is the British Government. A further corollary is that the British army and the PSNI are the *politically* legitimate army and Police of Northern Ireland.

The principle of consent is one of the few places where the Agreement is not ambiguous in its language. It is one of the reasons why accepting the Agreement was an enormous sacrifice for Republicans. Nonetheless most Republicans, when asked, deny the legitimacy of the British Government and army, and to a lesser extent, the PSNI, although they accept all three as being facts on the ground.

The distinction between *political* and *moral* legitimacy is important. It is difficult to see how any Republican could accept the moral legitimacy of the British Government in Northern Ireland. They are therefore committed to changing that situation. However, one can coherently accept the *political* legitimacy of a government while rejecting its *moral* legitimacy, or the moral legitimacy of many of its actions. For example, one can condemn a particular taxation policy as immoral because of its impact on the poor while continuing to pay taxes as one worked to change the policy. One can accept as legitimate an ambassador from a particular country, while at the same time condemning that country's human rights abuses and seeking to change its government.

The critical issue is one of showing respect for the symbols of government. Would it be contradictory for Republicans to show respect for the Union Jack, accept it as the flag of the country, while at the same time being committed to working for a United Ireland? The answer is No. Standing for the British national anthem can be a mark of respect for British people in Northern Ireland, a recognition that the British Government is the *politically* legitimate Government for the time being, without suggesting that one is not committed to changing this.

The same arguments can be put about showing respect for the British monarchy, although Irish Nationalists, like British Republicans, are opposed to the monarchy.

Clearly an agreed Northern Ireland would be a difficult compromise for Republicans, a step too far in the view of many, given the changes they have already accepted. Yet the proposal does not contradict any key republican principle. It respects the right of the people of Ireland to self-determination because they can exercise this right by choosing this option if they wish. It is therefore democratic. It is not an internal solution because an agreed Northern Ireland can exist in the context of a United Ireland. It is more likely to win the acceptance of the unionist community than a unitary state. It would therefore have a higher chance of contributing to peace on the whole island.

There is an onus on Unionists to show respect for the symbols of Nationalists and Republicans because, willy-nilly, they are part of the people of Northern Ireland. There cannot be an agreed Northern Ireland without tolerance by Irish people of British symbols and institutions, and a tolerance by British people of Irish symbols and institutions. Further, Unionists cannot expect Republicans to accept the principle of consent if they do not do so themselves. That means committing themselves to accepting the terms of the Agreement: if 50% plus, North and South, choose a United Ireland then the two Governments will work together to bring this about. Unionists need to show they are committed to accepting this without resorting to violence if it should ever happen.

A Northern Ireland identity within the UK, Ireland and Europe
Northern Ireland has an existing communal identity, but we do not see it because we emphasise our separate identities. There are no symbols to support our shared identity, yet it continues to exist. We can write down all the things that separate us because they are visible, but we cannot spell out the things we share in common. Nevertheless the Agreement could not have been made without this shared experience. One example is the pain of our experience of the Troubles. We also have a common language, political administration, school curriculum, similar faiths (at least they seem that way to outsiders), shared working-class problems and a dark sense of humour. The British in Northern Ireland differ from other British people because they are influenced more by Irish identity. The Irish differ from other Irish people because they are influenced more by a British identity (at least the Northern Ireland version of British identity).

Part of the task involved in committing ourselves to the people of Northern Ireland, to the territory of Northern Ireland, and to the principle of consent as the only mechanism by which any move might be made towards a United Ireland, is to recognise and develop what we share in common. It would be interesting to see what would happen if all the parties in Northern Ireland were asked to spell out their values in detail. How many of their most important values would they hold in common?

Developing a shared Northern Ireland identity needs to go hand in hand with finding ways to deepen our connections with Britain, the Republic and the EU. Each of these can help take the focus off our differences. There is no reason why we cannot do this. Connections have shifted dramatically over the centuries and will continue to do so in the future. For thousands of years up to the start of the 20th century people in the Northern third of Ireland had closer connections with Scotland than with the rest of Ireland. The Scottish connections are still strong for many Protestants, less so now for Catholics.

The European Community will be central to Northern Ireland's existence in the future, as it has been increasingly since both the UK and Ireland joined in 1973 - almost a generation ago. This will happen whether or not people in Northern Ireland agree. In 2004 over 70% of legislation passed in both the UK and Ireland was required because of EU regulations.

Unionists have a more negative attitude than Nationalists to the EU. The UUP opposed the European Constitution and the UK adoption of the Euro. The EU is not a panacea, but the only way Northern Ireland will maximise its gains from Europe is by Unionists and Nationalists working together. Northern Ireland MEPs have often done so, but this is seldom emphasised.

Only if the politicians work together will the people of Northern Ireland make an effective contribution to Europe. The new EU, with the addition of ten new States who joined on 1 May 2004 - Poland, Hungary, the Czech Republic, Slovakia, Slovenia, Latvia, Estonia, Lithuania, Cyprus and Malta - has many minorities caught in majority States. With our experience of our double minority, of trying to move from paramilitarism to constitutionalism, of developing human rights as a benefit for all and not a threat, of working to respect diversity, of seeking ways to deal with employment imbalances, we surely can offer a contribution to others.

SCENARIO TWO: A DIVIDED NORTHERN IRELAND

A second scenario is that we stay divided in Northern Ireland. We remain in our separate camps. We look for gains for our own group and may take a certain pleasure if this can be achieved at the expense of the others. We have two different understandings of the past, the present and the future.

One view sees the past as a struggle against terrorists, the other sees it as freedom fighters struggling against oppression. One sees the present as a messy, and polluting acceptance of criminals into government, something which might just about be acceptable if they ceased their criminal activity. The other sees it as an oppressed people slowly gaining justice through the political power which is their right because of their democratic electoral success.

One view sees Northern Ireland remaining as part of the UK. Many who hold this view hope that we will be able to maintain British values but fear that we are heading into a United Ireland. Others see us heading in that direction - without any precise picture of what this might involve.

The differences fought over are issues like inquiries into the past, the acceptability of the Police, the presence of the British army, flags and symbols, the routeing of parades, fair employment, the existence of the role of paramilitaries, Republicans accused of terrorism in Columbia, abuses in Castlereagh, collusion, funding for Irish and Scots-Irish languages, painted kerb stones and a hundred others. Just as one issue seems to be sorted out, we can be sure others will emerge. Others, who do not see themselves as either Unionists or Nationalists, continue to be politically marginalised.

A divided Northern Ireland does not necessarily rule out devolved government. It is quite conceivable that this will return because the political parties want it, but at the same time the basic divisions in Northern Ireland continue. Many hope that devolution might over time lead to a breaking down of these divisions, but there is no guarantee of this. In the context of continued divisions there will be pressure from Unionists and Republicans to retain designation in the Assembly. This means that each Member of the Assembly (MLA) is required to designate him or herself as a Unionist, Nationalist, or Other. Many argue that this simply reinforces sectarianism.

In a divided Northern Ireland fears among both Unionists and Nationalists are higher. Consequently it is more difficult to persuade loyalist or republican paramilitaries to close down their organisations. 'Punishment beatings', murders and crime are more likely to continue. In this context Northern Ireland will certainly not be a shining example to the world of a people who have overcome historical divisions.

Northern Ireland has been divided since the day it was set up in 1920. Segregation increased in the period after the Agreement and there was anecdotal evidence that sectarianism also increased. There was no sign of change over basic divisions in the short term, with the exception that an agreement between the DUP and Sinn Féin over devolved government seemed at least possible. For these reasons the more likely scenario for the forseeable future is a divided Northern Ireland.

A divided Northern Ireland may seem the more obvious future scenario, but if this turns out to be the case it will be costly. The funds we spend on conflict, for example on policing, reduce the budget available for other areas. Up to 2004 the UK Government paid the bills. This was always the case during the Troubles: those who lost their property in explosions were able to turn to the NIO, however long it took for compensation to arrive. It is not clear that this will always be the case. There was great sympathy for Northern Ireland because of the emergence of the peace process. But outsiders have grown increasingly tired of it as it has dragged on. In that context it would not be surprising if the British Government, subtly or otherwise, made Northern Ireland pay more of the bill for the cost of the Troubles or for the failure to work together.

Some argue that this might not be a bad thing as the pressure might lead to positive outcomes. They point to examples where the pressure of funding has led to change elsewhere: in the late 1990s the US Congress could not agree on a Federal Budget. The consent of both the Senate and the House of Representatives was necessary. At the end of the financial year the salaries of federal employees were stopped. This lasted for about six weeks. Then the politicians compromised. They had to: the cost of not doing so would have been too high politically.

If the UK Government paid a proportion of the subsidy for Northern Ireland only with cross-community consent in the Assembly, and if the absence of such consent meant this element of the subsidy would not be forthcoming, then it is more likely that Northern Ireland politicians would find a way to compromise. In 2004 this incentive was missing.

SCENARIO THREE: A UNITED IRELAND

As already mentioned, in the 1998 Agreement the two Governments agreed to set in motion steps to bring about a United Ireland if the majority, North and South, voting in separate referenda, agreed. These referenda would only be put if the two Governments took the view that they were likely to succeed.

In 2001 over 40% of Protestants thought a United Ireland was either 'quite likely' or 'very likely' according to the *Northern Ireland Life and Times Survey*. This figure had changed little since 1998. In Community Dialogue events many Unionists said they believed a United Ireland was inevitable, that this would be forced upon them and that their identity in a United Ireland would not be respected. Many Republicans also said they saw a United Ireland as inevitable. The Life and Times Survey shows a change among Catholics: in 1998 10% thought a United Ireland was 'very likely' and 35% 'quite likely'. By 2001 this had shifted to 15% thinking it was 'very likely' and 29% 'quite likely'.

In the context of a divided Northern Ireland the issue of a United Ireland was likely to heighten Unionists' fears and increase Nationalists' expectations.

However, there were factors which made it unlikely that a United Ireland would emerge in the forseeable future:

- The 2001 census showed Catholic numbers were stabilising and were unlikely to exceed Protestant numbers for many years.
- Even if there were a majority of Catholics they would not all vote for a United Ireland (surveys showed 15%-20% of Catholics did not want a United Ireland as their first choice).
- Many argued that the majority of the people of Northern Ireland were in favour of staying within the UK and had a moral right to do so.
- Many also argued that changing the current situation in which one community - Nationalists - are denied membership of their country of choice to another situation in which Unionists are denied the country of their choice did not seem like a good idea.

There were a range of practical difficulties which would have to be addressed before a United Ireland could emerge.

Political issues
- Would Northern Ireland remain as a political unit? If so, would the same power-sharing arrangements continue?
- Would British people be able to maintain their British identity? Would they be able to swear allegiance to the Monarch? Would they be able to fly the Union flag? If so, when and where?
- Would there be any political connection between the Republic and the UK?
- Would current members of the Dáil - the Irish parliament - be willing to create new seats to allow for extra numbers from the North, or would they agree to reducing the number of seats, thereby possibly lessening their own chances of election?
- Would the electorate in the Republic support unity if Unionists were opposed to it?
- Would the two Governments support unity given the likely instability which would follow? The experience of border changes in the Europe since World War II (former Yugoslavia, the Czech Republic and Slovakia, East and West Germany) while mixed, has enough negative factors to advise against a change. West Germany's union with the East made a major negative impact on the country's economy.

Security and policing
- Would the Irish army take over from the British army as the back-up to the Police in Northern Ireland? How would this work

in loyalist areas?
- Would there be a separate police force for Northern Ireland?
- Would it be under the authority of a Southern Minister?
- Would the Northern Ireland Policing Board be retained?

Finance
- How would the British Government's subsidy be replaced? It is important to note that this would be a much larger proportion of total government expenditure in the case of the Republic than that of the UK.

Administration
- Would the various government departments be integrated?
- Would there still be Northern Ireland departments under the authority of central government departments of the Republic? If they were to be integrated how big a problem would this be?
- Where current differences in practice between North and South exist which alternative would be adopted?

Education
- Would the Republic continue to insist on Northern Ireland primary-school teachers passing an examination in Irish? Would this be extended to other schools?
- What impact would unification make on integrated education, or on Protestant-only schools?

The above questions give some idea of how complex a task it would be to bring about a United Ireland. There were other reasons which made it unlikely:
- Governments tend to be slow to make major changes without compelling reasons which are clearly beneficial to themselves.
- Both Governments are happy to see the conflict confined to Northern Ireland and avoiding major constitutional change is the best way to keep it that way.
- The vast majority of Unionists and about 15-20% of Catholics seem happy with the status quo.
- If the Assembly gets up and running again Nationalists will probably be less disaffected in Northern Ireland and may therefore be willing to tolerate continued membership of the UK.
- The British Government cannot remove Northern Ireland from the UK without the consent of the majority, North and South. This is partly because of the Agreement but also because it

would be politically impossible for a UK Government to expel one of the four countries of the UK (England, Scotland, Wales and Northern Ireland) from the UK against the will of the majority of that country. To do so would be opposed on constitutional grounds among others.

However, it is worth noting that unifications have taken place when there were practical arguments against them: the fact that West Germany was likely to suffer economically from union with the East did not block the moves to unity. This shows the extent to which issues like this are decided by political will.

The fact that a United Ireland is unlikely does not rule out increased North-South cooperation. The needs of health, security, finance, agriculture, education and other areas are likely to drive both North and South in that direction. For instance, it is neither sensible nor necessary to allow new health initiatives to be held back by state borders, and already there has been some movement on this: NHS patients who have been kept on a waiting list for a certain time now have the right to treatment in other EU countries if it is available. This trend is likely to increase. If devolved government is restored in Northern Ireland then the Executive will oversee the Northern side of this. In the absence of devolution the Northern side will be controlled by Westminster.

Secondly, the EU already makes a major impact on both the law and the economy in Northern Ireland. This also is likely to increase. If conflict is reduced people may have more energy to focus on European issues.

Finally, there is one special factor which may increase movement towards an agreed Northern Ireland. If the Executive is restored and survives for the long-term new alliances among the parties within Northern Ireland will emerge. This will happen inevitably because of the horse trading necessary to do on-the-ground politics. The longer this continues people will get used to a new Northern Ireland. Gradually this may lead to greater agreement. It is possible, and even likely, that the level of agreement, leading to practical cooperation, will be far greater than any individual party will care to admit in their formal statements.

TASKS FOR ALL SCENARIOS

Institutions
In the absence of agreement the British Government may look

sympathetically at other proposals. In 2004 the DUP proposed a form
of government by the Assembly. The SDLP suggested having ten non-
political individuals appointed by the two Governments to run the
Northern Ireland departments while being accountable to the
Assembly. The ten would include one nominee each from the EU and
the Republic. The party argued that it was better to have some
element of devolution than none at all. Both parties argued that the
limitations of their proposals would be an incentive to all sides to work
for agreement so that the Executive could be restored.

The system of designation was being questioned by some in the lead
up to the negotiations in the Autumn. Under this, each MLA chose to
be designated as a Unionist, Nationalist, or Other. This was the basis
of further rules under the Agreement about sufficiency of consensus:
important measures needed majority approval of both Unionists and
Nationalists, or else 40% of each together with 60% overall. Originally
the aim of this was to protect Nationalists. The Alliance Party argued
that dropping designation and requiring 60%-plus approval for
important measures was preferable, because it opened the possibility
of moving away from sectarian blocs.

While the Executive was running many were critical of the degree
of autonomy given to Ministers. While each department had a
committee, Ministers could act independently of it. The DUP also
abused the conventions of cabinet responsibility by refusing to attend
meetings at which Sinn Féin were present. A further problem was that
there was little pressure on a Minister who performed badly. Nor was
his or her party likely to suffer at the polls because these were
dominated by internal unionist or nationalist feuds, not by ministerial
performance. Under the Agreement only the party concerned could
remove a Minister and it then had the right to nominate a
replacement. A mechanism was needed to ensure ministerial
responsibility.

Paramilitarism

Republicans: Republicans faced a key question: would the IRA stand
down before a United Ireland was achieved? This was obviously a
major issue for them. Yet without disbandment the contradiction
between Republicans being in government and the IRA existing was
highlighted by the question: what does the IRA exist for? As a
paramilitary group its purpose was to kill or be prepared to kill people.
But who were its targets? The British army? The security forces?
Loyalists? Dissident Republicans? (All but the latter were excluded

under the 1994 cessation). If the IRA was not there to kill people why did it exist?

One argument was that its purpose was to defend nationalist areas since these could not rely on the Police. But how were they to defend these areas if they could not kill those attacking them? A response was that the fear of being killed kept Loyalists at bay. There was undoubtedly an element of truth in this, but against this the existence of the IRA was politically destabilising and this in turn created a political context in which loyalist attacks were more likely. Again a response to this was that the wider political viewpoint is all right for analysts, but it is not much use at three o'clock in the morning if a person's house is being attacked and they know the Police will not turn up to protect them. This shows the chicken and egg nature of the debate: the Police would be more likely to turn up if they were less afraid and had more resources. Both these would be more likely in the absence of paramilitaries. But even the best police force in the world will not be able to give 24 hour cover to the whole community.

An issue for Republicans was the alleged involvement of the IRA in crime. Some Republicans deny this and attribute charges of criminality down to securocrats in the security forces. Undoubtedly these exist, but so also does IRA crime, for example so-called punishment beatings. This was justified as 'internal house-keeping' and as a response to community demands. The question can be asked 'internal' to what? A response to what community? This brings us back to the question of the political, as distinct from moral, legitimacy of the State. If Republicans do not recognise the political legitimacy of the State, then why are they trying to get into the government of that State?

Further questions arose concerning republican links to crime: were Republicans themselves happy with IRA involvement in smuggling and other crime? Was this why the IRA was founded? What happened to the proceeds of these crimes? If they did not go to Sinn Féin, as Republicans said, did they simply go into the pockets of those carrying out these crimes? If so, this was a change for the IRA. In the past members doing that would have been in severe difficulties.

Republicans therefore faced a choice: they could either allow IRA activity to continue and face both the political cost of this and the further moral undermining of their movement. Or they could decide that this phase of the conflict was truly over, that the future lay in constitutional politics - with all its limitations - and act to end IRA activity. This would have involved addressing at least all the areas listed in Article 13 of the Joint Declaration of the two Governments, 'including military attacks, training, targeting, intelligence gathering, acquisition or development of arms or weapons, other preparations for terrorist campaigns, punishment beatings and attacks and involvement in riots. Moreover, the practice of exiling must come to an end and the exiled must feel free to return in safety. Similarly, sectarian attacks and intimidation directed at vulnerable communities must cease' *(http://www.nio.gov.uk/pdf/joint2003.pdf, April 2003).*

But it should go beyond this to include an end to all involvement in crime, despite Bertie Ahern's statement in 2004 that the two Governments had decided not to include smuggling in the list.

The alternative for Republicans is to decide to maintain what is in effect a State within a State. This would mean that they would continue to raise funds through IRA activity and to 'police' republican areas. They would deny in public any links between Sinn Féin and the IRA, and they would seek either to be included in a devolved government in Northern Ireland, or else to use their influence on the two Governments in the context of Direct Rule. Increasingly, however, non-Republicans questioned why they should go along with this.

Loyalists: Loyalists had little chance of making political progress among the Protestant community both because the Protestant community as a whole was less forgiving of paramilitaries and because during the Troubles Loyalists fought to defend the Union and did not develop any other major political aims. But they had the possibility of making an impact in the Community Sector. If they chose to do so while continuing as paramilitaries, however, they undermined the basis of their community work.

Loyalists presented themselves primarily as defenders of their people against the IRA. The facts did not support this. Loyalist violence exceeded that of Republicans between 2002 and 2004.

If the purpose of Loyalists was to defend their community against republican attack, what purpose did they have in the context of a ceasefire? Many in the loyalist community worked to transform loyalism. The central question they faced was the same as that facing Republicans: what is the moral and political basis of a paramilitary group in a democratic society?

Finally there was an important difference between Loyalists and Republicans: the former were much more divided than the latter.

Policing
Sinn Féin said its members would join the Policing Board 'when we

have got policing right', but the problem was that we were never going to get policing 'right'. The Police are asked to act on behalf of society to prevent crime, arrest criminals and use minimum force in doing so. But the Police is an organisation of human beings. It will always suffer from bureaucratic and personal failures. The best way to change the Police is from the inside. The ethos of police officers themselves will always be the major determinant of behaviour. Next to that, the Board can influence things. By taking its place on the Board Sinn Féin would not only be committing itself to the Northern Ireland of the future, it would also be helping to create it. This could be done without prejudice to any long-term goal of a United Ireland.

Agreement about the past
As we discussed in Chapter Three, there are only a number of ways to handle the past and all have their disadvantages. If Unionists and Nationalists were to commit themselves together to Northern Ireland they would need to find a way to handle the past which both could live with. Central to this would be acceptance that the past need not define the present or future of a person or a group. This is obvious because people and groups change, but often that change is not recognised by others. Sometimes this is because these do not want to let go of the past. Sometimes they believe the person has not really changed because they see too many similarities between their past and present actions. Either of these reasons is enough to have a major negative impact on the possibility of Unionists and Nationalists moving forward together.

We cannot resolve issues from the past: it was too brutal, painful and messy for this. We have to be willing to live together in a way in which the past no longer dominates our lives or prevents us from working with those who were our enemies. An agreed Northern Ireland would represent a commitment to face the future together. It would not mean forgetting the past, or even necessarily agreeing on how to handle it. However, the context of an agreed future would make disagreement about the past easier to live with.

In the light of the above it is worth asking ourselves about the new energy and resources which would be available to us if we had an agreed Northern Ireland. In 2004 the Republic of Ireland, which held the Presidency of the EU for six months, was centrally involved in winning agreement among the other 24 States for an EU Constitution. While this was happening some of the things we in Northern Ireland were concerned with were: Republicans in Columbia, the Independent

Monitoring Commission report on paramilitarism, the killing of senior
Loyalist Brian Stewart in East Belfast (18 May 2004), loyalist pipe
bomb attacks on a Sinn Féin worker in Ballymena, amnesties for the
'On the Runs', early release for the killers of Garda Jerry McCabe, IRA
involvement in smuggling and the question of where the money goes,
the threat of increased interface violence in the summer, and threats
over new housing developments in North Belfast. Imagine if none of
these was the focus of our attention because we had agreed about the
future. What then could we contribute to making Northern Ireland a
new society? What could we contribute to other European and Third-
World countries?

Cooperation among Churches
There was a steady decline in the number of people who attended
Church in Northern Ireland between 1989 and 2001:
  · Roman Catholics: 63% (down from 86% in 1989),
  · Church of Ireland: 30% (down from 35% in 1989)
  · Presbyterian: 37% (down from 45% in 1989) (*Northern Ireland
    Life and Times Survey*, 2001).

Nonetheless these figures showed a considerable proportion of the
population were involved in Churches.
    The best way for Churches to lead is by example. Calls to the rest
of society to cooperate while Churches do so to only a limited extent
were always going to fall on deaf ears. There was increased cooperation
and a reduction in tension between many Churches in the period after
the Agreement. Good work was done on mixed marriages, clergy
groups were more relaxed with each other, the clergy in Omagh
showed joint leadership in the aftermath of the 1998 bomb. The
Church of Ireland worked on sectarianism. The Presbyterian Church
appointed peace workers. Nonetheless Churches managed to keep
themselves entirely separate on almost every Sunday in the year
despite the Lord's prayer at the Last Supper 'that they may be one'
(John 17). The bulk of church effort still went into creating separate,
not united, communities. If Churches are to make a greater positive
contribution to a future Northern Ireland, this will need to change.
This can only happen if building relationships becomes a priority in
man and woman hours and other resources.
    Churches regularly condemn violence. However, they have no basis
to do so in a self-righteous way, both because this is against Gospel
values (cf. the story of the Pharisee and the Publican), and also

because of the wrongs committed by the Churches themselves during the Troubles, above all by helping to foster strong but segregated communities.

In 2004 there was no indication that segregation in Northern Ireland was going to decline. The existence of groups which are both segregated and also lack understanding of each other is a bad formula on which to build a political future. This is why Community Dialogue believes on-going, deeper and more widespread dialogue is essential.

Sectarianism and racism

Cecilia Clegg and Joe Liechty (*Moving Beyond Sectarianism*, Columba, 2001) have argued that sectarianism is a good impulse among people seeking community but it is an impulse which has gone wrong. People need community and will always build it. But in Northern Ireland because of fear and other factors we have built segregated work, faith, leisure and housing communities. Many suspect that sectarianism has deepened since the ceasefires. Certainly segregation increased in the years following the Agreement. The problem is not simply one of segregation - there are many examples in other countries of segregated groups not being in conflict - but segregation allied to other factors, such as, conflict over land, real and perceived discrimination, and violence. If violence ceased and if we had a widespread commitment to an agreed Northern Ireland it might be possible to tackle sectarianism effectively. It is difficult to see us making a serious inroad into the problem in the absence of these changes.

The statement is often made - and believed by many Nationalists - that Loyalists are more sectarian than Republicans. The issue of sectarianism is complex. Technically sectarianism is a particular brand of prejudice, one deeply influenced by religion. The question, therefore, is not are Loyalists more prejudiced than Nationalists, but are they more prejudiced in a particular way, i.e. one particularly influenced by religion?

A range of reasons are given by Loyalists for denying the charge that they are more sectarian:

- They had a military reason to kill Catholics and this was why they did so, not for sectarian reasons. (This has parallels with the republican argument that they killed members of the security forces because they were military targets, not because they were mostly Protestants).
- Those who concede sectarianism among their fellow travellers argue that Republicans are just as sectarian, but in their case it

is dressed up as ideology.
- Republicans stopped killing Protestants because the British Government made so many concessions to them.
- Republican opposition to Orange parades was blatantly sectarian and this opposition was deliberately fomented by Republicans throughout Northern Ireland. This was part of an orchestrated attack against Protestant culture as a whole.
- Many Loyalists saw this as an attempt to provoke them into attacking Republicans and/or Catholics generally.
- Loyalist community workers for the most part claimed to have been able to persuade people not to respond. These workers also encouraged young Loyalists to enjoy their own culture in their own areas, thereby drawing them away from interface areas. It was a long, hard lesson for Loyalists to learn that responding to republican provocation plays into the hands of Republicans.

Some of the contrary arguments are:
- Loyalists continued to kill Catholics after republican killings had virtually ceased. This suggests at least that sectarianism remained strong in many loyalist circles. (It may be that this comment does not apply to some loyalist organisations because such killings were not authorised at leadership level, or that the loyalist organisations were less centralised than republican groups and therefore had less control over what their members did).
- Fundamentalist Protestant Churches are more strongly anti-Catholic than the Catholic Church is anti-Protestant (Catholic prejudice is more likely to be political). While most Loyalists have little contact with Churches, nonetheless the views of Protestant fundamentalists can permeate the wider community.
- Many Loyalists hate everything to do with the Catholic Church. For some this may be because they still believe (incorrectly) that the Catholic Church, as such, hates Protestants. (Many Nationalists also hate the Orange Order because they see it as anti-Catholic. Orangemen point out that they are opposed to the teaching of the Roman Church, not to Catholics as individuals).

There are some other reasons why there might be more sectarianism in loyalist than in nationalist areas:
- Sectarianism tends to break out in loyalist areas in which the population is dwindling and which are near expanding

nationalist areas. It can therefore be seen as a community response to what is seen as a threatening situation. It happens more in loyalist than in nationalist areas because the loyalist areas are declining in numbers.

- Racism is a separate but related issue and it may also have been a factor in the increased number of racist attacks in loyalist areas in 2004: because their numbers were declining more people from ethnic minorities may have moved into loyalist areas and then been faced with the deep insecurities of the community.

These comments suggest that social insecurity lies at the root of both sectarianism and racism.

In 2004 there were a series of racist attacks on ethnic minorities in the Donegal Road area of Belfast. A survey showed that Northern Ireland was the most racist region of the UK. Racism is not new in Northern Ireland. For decades Travellers have been subjected to discrimination, as were Boat People from Vietnam from the 1980s. Dealing with racism means helping people to come to terms with diversity and to see it not as a threat but as a gift. It means recognising that human beings of all colours, class, creed and background need to respect one another. It would be sad if we ended a conflict based on British and Irish nationalisms and religion, and replaced it with one based on race. An agreed Northern Ireland would not simply be a place for Unionists and Nationalists, but for the many ethnic groups already settled here, and the thousands of Northern Ireland-born people who see themselves as neither unionist nor nationalist.

At the same time in 2004 as the attacks in loyalist areas, Féile an Phobail, the West Belfast Festival, organised by Republicans, Nationalists and others celebrated the diverse groups living in the area. It was easier for Republicans to do this than Loyalists because they were an expanding and more confident community and were not facing the same decline in numbers as Loyalists. Nor is racism absent from nationalist or republican areas. Nonetheless racism is an issue the loyalist community needs to address urgently.

Social issues
A 2003 report commissioned by Democratic Dialogue, a Northern Ireland think-tank, found 'that half a million people live in poor households in Northern Ireland, that these include 37 per cent of all children, that inequality is more severe than in the Republic of Ireland

and significantly worse than in Britain, and that it appears to be rising' (*Bare Necessities: Poverty and Social Exclusion in Northern Ireland-Key Findings*, info@democraticdialogue.org). These shocking figures highlight again the tragedy involved in diverting energy and resources to constitutional issues when these could be focused on issues like poverty.

Northern Ireland is no different from anywhere else in that it suffers from the destruction of the environment. Focus on our divisions has distracted attention from this. Clearly work on the environment will benefit people in Northern Ireland, but it is also an area in which people here can make a vital contribution to the future of the planet by cooperating with other countries.

Segregated housing is a symptom of fear. It also causes fear because when people are separated they do not get to know each other and this in itself may cause more fear. In turn, this leads to myths and stereotypes remaining unchallenged. Problems are blamed on the other group. They tend to be seen as better-off, and there is a widespread belief that they get better funding grants.

As with all our other problems there is no easy answer to the problem of segregated housing. Former paramilitaries again can play a crucial role. If they decided to support mixed housing it would become a more realistic possibility. Mixed housing involves creating space, not only for Unionists and Nationalists to live together, but also for ethnic minorities. The group which suffers most from discrimination is Travellers. Working-class areas are more segregated than leafy suburbs, so community groups and individuals active in these areas can help increase tolerance of wider diversity.

Progress towards mixed housing could potentially lead to an increase in the number of integrated schools. This would enable neighbouring children from mixed backgrounds to attend the same school, instead of the current situation in which a few children from different areas are bussed to integrated schools.

In the absence of devolution British Ministers will rule Northern Ireland directly. This will make effective work on social issues more difficult. With or without an Executive the Government needs to recognise and fund the role of the Community Sector. European funding has been cut because it was meant as a limited injection to help the peace process. But building a new society in Northern Ireland is a long-term project. Without funding, the Community Sector cannot continue to play a key role. Without its work the problem of racism and sectarianism will deepen, more people will be economically marginalised, the misuse of alcohol and other drugs will grow. Given this, it is extraordinary that a government should support the business community with vast subsidies yet at the same time minimise the role of the Community Sector.

Change is inevitable
The one prediction which can be made with certainty about the future is that some things will change radically. The unionist and nationalist communities of 2004 have changed significantly from those of 1984. The same will be true in 2024. Some of these changes are foreseeable, some not. It is natural for human beings to want to hold on to the familiar.

One likely change is increased immigration, especially from countries which joined the EU in 2004, and particularly in the first fifteen years or so of their membership as their economies catch up with the rest of Europe. This will impact on Northern Ireland communities. Already in 2004, 10% of the population of Dungannon were Portuguese. Some people opposed racist attacks on the grounds that those attacked made a positive contribution to the Northern Ireland economy. In fact, whether or not they make a contribution, citizens of all countries that were members of the EU in 2004 will have a human, moral and legal right to live and work in any other EU country by 2011 at the latest.

Other changes will come from technology, such as the internet, global markets and threats to security.

British and Irish Nationalism
One likely but uncertain change will be in nationalism, both British and Irish. The British State has changed dramatically with devolved government in Scotland, Wales and - fitfully - in Northern Ireland. The monarchy has been under threat. With the passing of Queen Elizabeth II this is likely to increase. These changes will inevitably impact on Unionists' sense of Britishness.

Irish nationalism has changed enormously since the start of the Troubles. Then the Irish Government laid claim to Northern Ireland (although it is disputed whether Articles II and III were a legal claim or legal limitation), the majority of Irish people were focussed on a territorial understanding of Irish unity, and there was little understanding of Unionists because few Southerners had met any. In Northern Ireland Nationalists saw themselves as second-class citizens and for the most part accepted this role. Now the two Governments have agreed that the problem should be seen as one of a double minority - Nationalists as a minority within Northern Ireland, Unionists a minority within the context of the island as a whole - and not as a colonial one. Nationalists no longer see themselves as second-class citizens, have participated in government, and at least 40% of them (SDLP voters) have accepted the legitimacy of the PSNI.

Increasingly it may become obvious that we have many overlapping identities - political, cultural, religious, gender, family and work. If all of these were to coincide with each other we would live only with those who share the same identities as ourselves in all of these areas. In the area of politics the 20th century has shown that in many instances the boundaries of the State will not coincide with the ethnic identity of a group. Many minorities are and will remain caught within States in which the majority 'ethnic' identity is different from their own. In time we may become more relaxed about this, provided that equality of respect is shown by the State to all identities.

Many of the ideas outlined in this section were discussed at length at Community Dialogue events. In the last chapter we will look at the process used to facilitate the dialogue.

5

Dialogue Theory and Practice

Introduction
Between 1998 and 2004 Community Dialogue ran over 500 events. The purpose of these was to encourage dialogue among people who disagreed deeply with each other about the past, present and future and who were hurting deeply because of the conflict. Our aim was understanding, not agreement. We believed that if groups understood each other more deeply they would be better able to make informed decisions about starting, continuing or ending conflict. If they stepped into the world of the other group and saw how these others came to hold their positions, feel their emotions and choose their values, then although the groups often remained opposed to each other, they were less likely to engage in violence. The questions discussed were highly emotive, but through the dialogue process people learnt more about the issues, dealt with them in a less emotive way, and slowly began to hear why other groups held the positions they did. In this chapter we look at how the Community Dialogue process worked and at some of the issues it raised.

Background
All our events were organised around three questions which we raised in one form or another:
  · What is it that you really want?
  · Why do you want it?
  · What can you live with?

We found that these questions, when considered within our ground rules for facilitated dialogue, helped people develop a deeper understanding of what really mattered both to themselves and to other groups. It also helped them to be more critical of what their own

125

politicians said.

Constantly in the dialogues people started with a fairly simple statement about political difficulties and then as others responded the picture became more complex. This was because the stories and experiences of participants emerged.

The understanding we hoped for was not simply clinical. We wanted it to be empathetic. This meant that, while continuing to disagree, they could see how in different circumstances they might have held the views, felt the emotions, had the values, and believed in the things that their opponents did. As a result of this many found they had more in common with their opponents than they realised, although a minority did not.

One example was that of a Loyalist and a Republican. Throughout the first day of a Community Dialogue residential the Loyalist did not say much. On the second day he was in a small group with the Republican and some young people. Towards the end of the session he said: 'I hope you young people don't think that just because I'm here with him (pointing to the Republican) that I find it easy'. And then he paused, looked at the Republican and said: 'And, come to think of it, I don't suppose he finds it easy either'. The Republican turned to him and replied 'No, I don't. But I'm glad you're here'. Then the two men shook hands.

That hand shake was important. It would be foolish to think that it signified agreement. Each remained a Republican or a Loyalist. Rather it was a sign of how difficult the process was for each of them. But by recognising this they recognised each other's humanity.

After several years we divided our work into stages: Stage One focussed on the immediate experience of dialogue. Stage Two involved reflecting both on the dynamics of the conflict and on the process of dialogue.

We see dialogue as quite separate from mediation or negotiation. Indeed we believed that it would be a block to dialogue if any of the participants thought it was connected with either. This was because dialogue is about exploring what really matters to an individual. In negotiations it is often important not to reveal this.

Ground rules
The ground rules for dialogue are important and all participants were asked to accept these as a condition of participation:
- There was no task to achieve.
- We were not hoping for or expecting agreement.

- The event took place in a safe space.
- It was confidential.
- People could change their mind about any issue.
- There was no need to convince anyone else of one's own views: no vote would be taken at the end of the event, nor any press statement issued.
- The most important question at the end would be: what questions arose for you?
- People were invited to share their experience of the Troubles if they wished. But if one shared there would be no pressure on others to follow suit.
- Participants were invited to search, not to look for or to defend certainty.
- The importance of respect and listening deeply to each other was stressed.
- Everyone attended as an individual, not as a representative of an organisation or a group.

Open-ended process

The process was open-ended. Many found this difficult. It goes back to the first of Community Dialogue's questions: 'What is it that really matters to you?' It would be contradictory to ask this question and then decide in advance on a topic for dialogue. For example, if we had asked people what it was that really mattered to them and then set decommissioning as the topic, we would be indicating that decommissioning was the thing that mattered most to them. In fact only the individual could decide what mattered most to him or her. That was why the open-ended approach was important. But it meant that at the beginning of the process a whole series of different issues came up as people slowly teased out which were the more important to them. During this time people stated positions and took up stances. It was only as the process advanced that they realised they did not need to hold on to these.

Scenario building

An important part of the process was to ask participants about the consequences of their position. An example was one group who wanted to strengthen the powers and armaments of the RUC, lift the legal restraints on them, and give them one focus: to lock up drug dealers. Exploring the consequences of this position exposed some of the difficulties with it - the dangers of a non-accountable police force, the need for legal process, likely community responses, etc - but it was up to the participants to decide whether or not they wanted to maintain their position.

Part of the scenario building involved asking: 'If you get what you really want, will you then be happy, or will you want something better?' or 'How will getting what you want impact on your day-to-day life?' This raised practical issues about health care, for example, either in the context of Northern Ireland remaining in the UK or joining a United Ireland.

The scenario building was only possible after initial positions had been laid out and defended, and after people began to talk at a deeper level about their experiences, values, emotions, fears and hopes. Working on scenarios earlier in the process would have led to more people simply defending their positions.

A further stage of the scenario building was to ask if there were alternative goals that appealed to people (it was up to participants, not facilitators, to suggest answers), or alternative ways to achieve these goals. This also opened up discussion of the likely consequences of the goals of other groups and whether alternatives were possible for them or not.

Scenario building touched on the interface between issues of identity (such as staying in the UK, moving to a United Ireland) and issues of interest (for example, better care for children). Weaving in and out of these were issues connected with the double minority thesis (Unionists feeling they were on a downward slope, Nationalists feeling they were looking for no more than their just rights).

Finally, towards the end of a Stage One dialogue it was sometimes possible to ask participants which of their desired goals could be attained only with the cooperation of the opposing group, what would be necessary to get that cooperation, and if they wanted to pay that price. Introducing these questions earlier would have been counter-productive. Even at the later stage, people tended to acknowledge the questions, but not deal with them in depth.

It is worth noting that much of the dialogue was about immediate day-to-day issues, such as policing, decommissioning, parades, identity, etc, and not the wider framework of the conflict. Because the political process was often stuck over one or more of these, many believed that the 1998 Agreement had already or would shortly fail. This view missed the distinction between structures internal to Northern Ireland which frequently failed and those which the two Governments controlled which continued to survive.

Dealing with symbols

Understanding the meaning of the other community's symbols was an important part of the dialogue. Day-to-day issues were seldom discussed on their own merits early in the dialogue but rather as symbols of one or other community's hopes, fears or resentments. Realising that symbols can mean different things to different groups helped: the one flag can stand for patriotism and be a deeply resented symbol of oppression at the same time.

Outcomes

Several things happened as a result of the Stage One dialogues. Participants became more comfortable and less defensive about their political position. They were able to see short-comings and difficulties in it. They were more open to listening to the position of others. In answering the questions, 'What is it that really matters to you?' and 'Why does it matter?' people explored their values, experiences and emotions. The process was slow but once people started on it they gained more confidence. Then a political position ceased to be a mere slogan and became instead something that had been examined. But also the values, experiences and emotions of others were listened to in a new way. Often this led to the desired outcome: not agreement, but understanding.

The dialogues were not only about individuals exploring their own deepest political desires. They were about listening to others - often enemies - doing the same. In the course of this many realised that their enemies believed what they said. They were not making it up, or saying it simply to annoy others, or as pure propaganda. This was an important change for several reasons: it led each side to take the other seriously and it raised the questions, 'Why do they believe what they do?', and 'What experiences brought them to this position?'

From the group to the individual

In the ground rules the focus was on the individual. Again and again we came back to our first question: 'What is it that really matters to you?' It often took over a day before participants began to hear that question, to realise that they did not have to stick to a party or group line, and to realise that we were not about to propose an answer to them. Indeed we were incapable of proposing an answer since the only expert on the question was the individual concerned. Once this was realised it was a transforming moment. For some it meant deconstructing politics, realising that some of what they had focussed on to date did not matter to them at a deep level, but that other parts did.

Focussing on the individual took the attention off the group identity and this eventually allowed space for people to examine how real or helpful their group ideology was. Our second question 'Why does it matter to you?' deepened the first. So, an individual might first say he or she wanted the British out of Ireland or else to maintain the Union with Britain. The 'why' question pushed the general statement back into more personal needs. The answer to this might be 'I want peace, security, education and respect for my identity and that of my children, and to be able to enjoy a feeling of belonging'. Each of these are important to most people, but they can all be obtained in a variety of ways. People sometimes responded to the 'why' question by saying they did not know why something mattered to them, but they were still clear that it did. This was not surprising. We can know what matters to us most of the time without being clear as to why.

The critical part of this phase of the dialogue was to help people get in touch with what it was that they really wanted.

From the individual to the group
We did not assume that if people were brought together they would automatically learn positive things about each other and that this would then lead to a change in stereotypes. Empirical studies indicate that this tends not to be the outcome of contact as such. Rather people create sub-groups of the stereotypes. So while they see another individual as a 'nice' Catholic or Protestant (and this is a change for them), they do not alter their negative stereotype of the other group as a whole. The Community Dialogue approach was closer to some form of Social Identity Theory which focuses on the reality that individuals categorize themselves as members of groups.

We hoped for a change in the way individuals understood other groups. In turn we hoped that if the participants were influential they would communicate this new understanding to others within their own group and this in turn would impact on their stereotypes. In practice this was likely to happen when a number of other factors were in place: progress at the political level, an absence of major contentious issues, and several local leaders having been involved in Community Dialogue or similar processes.

One outcome at a group level was that people learnt about the tensions within, and the limitations of, other communities. An example of this happened during one of the many occasions when the political process was blocked over 'guns and government'. Republicans were convinced that David Trimble was intent on humiliating them. In the course of a dialogue, however, Unionists made it clear that this was not the intention of most of their community. What mattered to them was getting an indication that Republicans were not going to return to violence once they had extracted concessions. Further, they believed that Trimble was on the edge in terms of surviving as leader. In that particular dialogue some progress was made in communicating both these realities to Republicans. However, Unionist participants during the dialogue did not really take on board the cost to Republicans of concessions which they had already made, for example, by taking office in a Government devolved from Westminster. Nor did they realise that this was the strongest possible evidence - within a republican framework - that the violence was over. For the most part Unionists also had no idea about divisions among Republicans. This was not surprising as only a small proportion of Unionists were willing to dialogue with Republicans or vice versa, and Republicans tended to keep their disputes within their movement.

The process also helped people to make more realistic comparisons between groups. Just as individuals need to present themselves positively so also do groups. The questions, 'What do I want?' and 'Why do I want it?' focussed on desires, not behaviour. If, and it was of course a big 'if', trust developed in the group the tendency to present idealised versions of one's own group was reduced. Often this happened most effectively in informal sessions.

In some cases the understanding confirmed negative views. One person said the process had proved that 'You can't talk to them'. In others the outcome was more positive. Either way the purpose was to give people more accurate data to assess the real perceptions and intentions of other groups, as well as giving them space to explore their own.

THE COMMUNITY DIALOGUE PROCESS: STAGE TWO

The Stage Two process involved cognitive analysis of both the peace process and the Community Dialogue method. Community Dialogue members and those who had taken part in many events were involved. So also was the Stanford Center on Conflict and Negotiation with whom we made a three year study on the theme of 'Reconciliation and Dialogue'. It is worth looking briefly at some of the points made about the main topics which came up and noting which were useful at Stage

One, and which were useful only in Stage Two dialogues. On all the topics, not untypically, there were a variety of viewpoints.

Understanding alone?
Should the aim of dialogue be understanding alone or should it also aim to build positive relationships? There was disagreement about this. Officially the organisation aimed at understanding alone, but some members wanted to go beyond this. A practical issue which arose from this was to ask how many times the same people should be invited to take part in dialogue. Those who saw the aim as understanding alone favoured inviting the same participants to a smaller number of events, giving them the opportunity to develop some understanding, and then moving on to new participants. Those who wanted to move beyond understanding favoured staying with the same participants and deepening the dialogue.

Relationships
It may seem obvious that the purpose of dialogue is to build relationships. In practice there were a variety of positions on this.

Some felt building inter-personal relationships between opponents had a ripple effect on the wider community. Others believed that this was not the case: what mattered was not a positive inter-personal relationship but an understanding of what went on in the other community so that this could be communicated to influential people within one's own community.

Some argued that the language of relationships was not appropriate in politics: who talks of a relationship with the tax man?

Others believed that it was important to focus on unionist-nationalist relationships because they were the protagonists. But against this it was noted that it was important to recognise they were not the only protagonists. The two Governments were also involved. Further, the one certainty we have about the future is that there will be change. Globalised economies, closer links in Europe, the virtual disappearance of the border between North and South (as with other borders in the EU) will all change things. How will this impact on Unionists and Nationalists? Will they still be recognisable entities in 10, 20 or 30 years time? Will focussing on them help block them from changing? Others pointed out that the 1998 Agreement was set up on the basis of Unionists and Nationalists. The first thing any new Assembly Member must do is designate him or herself as a Unionist, Nationalist, or Other. At least 40% support of both Unionists and

Nationalists is required for any contentious issue to be passed. Given the history of Northern Ireland neither group is likely to disappear in the near future.

Reconciliation
Some argued that reconciliation implied a previously existing relationship. This was not appropriate in Northern Ireland. 'Conciliation' was a more suitable term because Unionists and Nationalists had not previously had a positive relationship.

Another view was that reconciliation was used to mean so many different and opposing things that it was useless as a concept. Some of the different understandings of reconciliation were outlined in Chapter Three on the past. At times the term was also used for conflict management (keeping a lid on things), conflict resolution (removing the obstacles to an overall settlement), and conflict transformation (getting both sides to share a goal and work on it together). Each of these has a higher level of expectation. Community Dialogue members and participants differed greatly on which was an appropriate aim.

Some supported using reconciliation on the basis that if people have a positive experience of individuals on the other side they would change their view of the other community. As we have seen empirical evidence disputes this.

A further issue was tactical: participants in the early stages of our dialogues were often not attracted by reconciliation. They wanted to find ways to prove the other side wrong, or to show them how much suffering they had caused. In the light of this it was tactically better to keep discussion of reconciliation until later in the process.

Identity
The issue of identity figured a lot in our dialogues. The existence of Unionists and Nationalists as groups depends on their identity. In the case of Nationalists identity has been formed independently of, and often in opposition to, the State. With Unionists it has been different: their identity has been linked to the State in Northern Ireland, and central to this was seeing Northern Ireland as part of the UK. Interestingly, most Unionists at Community Dialogue events described themselves as Protestant, Ulster and British, and in that order. Although the first was a religious description it had links with the State. Historically Protestants believed the purpose of the State was to defend their religious liberties against Roman Catholic imperialism. At the start of the Troubles Unionists saw the British

Government as their friend. This changed, especially with the 1985 Anglo-Irish Agreement and later when Sinn Féin joined the Executive. The result was that Unionists were more likely to feel insecure in their identity than Nationalists.

Because republican identity was forged in opposition to the State there was a tension between being part of the Government and maintaining their identity. In the view of dissident Republicans the compromise meant the loss of their central values. Republicans were helped by being able to raise a series of issues on which they were still the rebels: enquiries into the past, refusal to join the Policing Board, opposition to Orange parades going through nationalist areas, etc. They also rejected the legitimacy of the State and symbolised this by refusing to fly the Union Jack over their Ministry buildings when in government. Yet the longer they stayed in government the more difficult it was to present themselves as rebels.

Loss

A consistent theme in our dialogues was that of loss, especially the unionist sense of loss. Some of this was due to diminished certainty: the unionist world was never as clear and well-defined as when the IRA were obviously outside the pale. Some of it was due to a sense that their identity was under threat. Some of it was because they felt Republicans were gaining and they were losing, although they were unclear about the details. This alienation of Unionists, and Republicans' frustration with it, impacted on the political process.

On the surface Unionists' sense of loss was somewhat surprising. As we have seen, they gained from the political process by virtue of the fact that Northern Ireland remained in the UK. Republicans on the other hand had to live with their aim of a United Ireland unfulfilled. They also gave up a central part of their ideology when they moved away from violence. They compromised by agreeing to tolerate and then to join a Northern Ireland Executive.

Republicans were far better at emphasising what they had gained and even packaging defeat as victory: they held a victory procession on the day the ceasefire was announced, and some youths scrawled 'Garda' (the title of the Police in the Republic) on the wall of the RUC barracks on Springfield Road in Belfast, although obviously the RUC had not moved out. Managing change was not easy for them, but they were better at it than the Unionists.

Ironically, the 2004 election which saw the triumph of the DUP, the arch-opponents of the Agreement, helped Unionists move away from alienation. In that election 'No' voters felt vindicated: they were no longer the moral outcasts. From that position of strength they may have felt better placed to negotiate with Sinn Féin. The strength of the No vote gave the pragmatists in the DUP more room for manoeuvre.

Unionists chose to present an idealised version of their past. A drawback of this is that the present always looks less attractive than the past. This makes it harder to sell any deal. Yet Loyalists make it clear that the past was not all rosy, and they regularly make the point that they suffered just as much from economic and social disadvantage as Nationalists did.

Groups regularly care more about what they lose than about what they gain. 'A deep mutual sense of loss pervades the aftermath of virtually every peace agreement in which there were no absolute victors' (Byron Bland, 'Getting beyond cheap talk', July 2004). One response to the issue of loss is to focus on the future and to point to the gains for everyone if bread and butter politics begin to dominate. But groups often continue to believe they have lost something important. The fact that they find it hard to specify what this is does not change the feeling. It is certainly related to realising that many things they took for granted no longer exist. In the unionist case they had lost a world in which there was never any question of Republicans being in government and in which they felt secure about Northern Ireland's future within the UK (even though the Agreement guarantees this as long as a majority favours it). In emphasising their loss Unionists were no different from other groups in similar situations who feel they have lost something of their civilization which they cannot specify, and the sense of loss induces fear and resentment in them.

In Community Dialogue's seminars and residentials it was sometimes helpful to ask participants in 'single identity' groups to a) remember the pain their group had suffered during the conflict and b) recall the pain suffered by the other group. They were then invited to share this with the other group. When a group articulated what the other group had suffered to the satisfaction of that group it normally made for a much more positive relationship between the groups, a willingness to listen to more of the other side's story, and a less defensive attitude about one's own side.

Open and closed Agreements
Unionists were willing to negotiate, but they did not want a settlement in which the other side would continue to come up with new demands. The closed settlement that they wanted, of course, included Northern

Ireland staying within the UK. Nationalists and Republicans for their part wanted an open agreement, one in which a broad framework would be agreed, but in which many things would be left vague and therefore open to further development. This included keeping open the option of a United Ireland.

There were parallels between this dynamic and that of other conflicts, notably the Middle East, where Jewish Israelis might have accepted a closed agreement, but Palestinians wanted one where issues like the right of return of refugees and the status of Jerusalem were left at least vague. This would mean that Palestinians could still dream about getting their land back. A closed agreement would take their dreams from them.

The political-community divide

A consistent theme in the dialogues was the gap and also the inter-relatedness between the peace process at the level of Northern Ireland politics and that at the local community level. The political level often impacted negatively on the community. But at times when things seemed to be going relatively well in the wider politics people on the ground complained that their basic problems remained the same. Further, one consequence of having new local politicians was that many of them thought they could fill the role of community leaders. They argued that they were elected, so it was up to them to represent the community. But the interests of the community always differed from those of party politics. A local issue, such as a parade, impacted negatively on wider politics. Alternatively, progress on it could make a positive impact on the wider scene. The Drumcree dispute in Portadown was a good example. The local dispute had existed for many years but it was made much worse by the change in the unionist-nationalist balance of power from 1994 on. In turn, the deepening of the local conflict impacted on the wider scene, when the RUC either blocked or forced an Orange parade through a nationalist area.

Participants in our dialogues often emphasised the work they were doing on the ground on contentious issues, by, for example, preventing trouble during parades, or developing mobile phone networks across interfaces. They felt they rarely got any credit for this. Other hotly-contested issues were the early release of prisoners, competition for housing in North Belfast, attacks by groups from either side at interfaces, and the issue of the past.

BARRIERS TO AGREEMENT

Our colleagues in Stanford University put forward a number of barriers to agreement. Some of these have already been mentioned. Some were useful in Stage One processes, while others only became relevant as we moved to Stage Two. They divided their list of barriers into those which blocked greater understanding and those which blocked better working relationships.

Barriers to greater understanding

Naïve realism: The features of this are that:
  (i)   People think the way they see the world is the way it actually is.
  (ii) If others are intelligent and fair-minded and had the correct data they would see the world as we do. This means that all we have to do is to meet them, explain the way things are to them and then they will agree with us.
  (iii) If this does not happen it will be either because they are stupid or bigoted. The result is that people will either walk away from dialogue, or else decide to go deeper.

An example is given by Padraig O'Malley commenting on the people he interviewed for *The Uncivil Wars: Ireland Today* (1983): 'All were utterly convinced of the righteousness of their own positions and invariably at a puzzled loss to understand "the other side's" failure to follow what to them was the simple, compelling logic of their own arguments'.

Obviously this was relevant to our dialogues. Normally participants became open to hearing what lay behind the positions of the other group only after they had begun to probe their own position more deeply and to realise that had they been exposed to different influences their own position would probably have been different.

False polarization: This is a tendency by disputants to assume that there is less common ground between them than is actually the case. Each side assumes the other is both more monolithic and more extreme than is actually the case. Each side fails to hear the uncertainties in the other's position.

One of the positive outcomes of some dialogues was that participants learnt much more about the internal tensions of the other community and realised they were nowhere near as monolithic as they had assumed. One example was Protestants learning that Catholics differ much more among themselves than they had expected.

Reactive devaluation: This means that once a concession is put on the table it is immediately devalued. The response in large part is due to distrust. We may want something badly but once our opponents offer it then the question arises: 'Why are they offering this now?' 'What's in it for them?' Were the same proposal put forward by a different group we might view it much more positively.

An example was that of changes to Articles II and III of the Republic's Constitution which was a unionist demand for many years. Once the change was made, as part of the 1998 Agreement, many Unionists felt the issue had not been that important.

These were useful ideas in Stage Two processes, but had they been raised in Stage One dialogues there would have been a temptation for participants to intellectualise them and thereby avoid some of the more basic emotional work which was needed.

Barriers to better working relationships

The Stanford group suggested four ideas under this heading:

The vision of a peaceful 'shared future': Often our vision of the future is one which excludes our enemies. Or else it includes them, but on our terms, which amounts to the same thing. So the question which arises is: 'What future would I find bearable, which my enemy would also find bearable?'

As we have seen, both Unionists and Nationalists wanted peace, but on their own terms. Each said they were including the other, but in each case the other felt excluded.

Open and closed agreements: Getting the balance on this is problematic because the group who are looking for change will always want the agreement to remain open. Those resisting change will want to ensure there are going to be no further changes. So, Unionists wanted to exclude all ambiguity from the Agreement, Nationalists to retain it.

Mutual acknowledgement of loss: We have mentioned this above. In the Northern Ireland context, Unionists managed to present themselves as having lost a lot, although arguably it was they who had gained most.

Justice: If either side to an agreement feels it is unjust they will simply look for an opportunity to change it in the future. If the parties have a similar idea of what justice is then there is a better chance they will arrive at a real agreement. Part of this involves trying to find out what the other side sees as a just entitlement and why.

We found we could constructively raise some but not all of these themes during or towards the end of a Stage One process. When participants were able to acknowledge mutual loss it was productive. Pointing out why it was entirely understandable that one side would want a closed and the other an open agreement was helpful towards the end of a dialogue. For the most part the issue of a shared future was resisted until well into 2004 when it began to be possible to raise it. Justice was a constant theme of the dialogues, but it tended to induce deafness as groups had opposing ideas of what it meant. Indeed Unionists felt the term had been hijacked by Republicans.

It was important that analytical work did not take place at Stage One. At the same time the insights people got about the peace process or about dialogue during Stage Two processes sometimes reminded them of experiences which they had blocked until then, and this allowed them deal with some of their more painful feelings. The differences between Stages One and Two are therefore important but not absolute.

Having gone through Stage One, participants were more open to criticising their own group both among themselves and with people from other communities. They recognised the limits of political rhetoric and also began to talk about the wider limits of what is likely to be achieved in politics. South Africa was an example we used in this context: the struggle against apartheid did not free millions of South Africans from poverty. This highlights the gap between political ideals and outcome. This also led to discussions about the wider context in which Northern Ireland operated: the EU, global economics, the power of the US, and by 2004 we were beginning slowly to ask questions about how people in Northern Ireland might make a positive contribution to overcoming conflict elsewhere.

CONCLUSION

At the end of the summer of 2004 there were conflicting predictions about what would happen in the political process. Gerry Adams raised the possibility of the IRA disbanding in the right context, and of Republicans joining the Policing Board if policing were devolved to Northern Ireland in the near future. In itself this was not new because 'the right context' was never spelt out. In one statement he said the British 'had to remove the unionist veto'. This was particularly unclear because Unionists had a veto on the process not only because of their political and military power, but also because the Agreement gives them one, as it does to Nationalists. Adams was reported as saying that disbandment would only happen when Tony Blair and the Irish Government gave cast-iron guarantees that the Agreement would be forced through against the wishes of intransigent Unionists. That can only be done in regard to matters which fall into the remit of the two Governments, or to a lesser extent in regard to North-South issues. Neither Government has the power to impose a devolved Executive, unless they fundamentally change the rules of the Agreement by dropping the requirement of the approval of both Unionists and Nationalists for major proposals.

Sinn Féin statements always contained ambivalent elements in them. As we have seen, ambivalent language was useful at different times to all the parties. Towards the end of the peace process its usefulness declined. Obviously Adams could not be specific about Sinn Féin's intentions in advance of the September 2004 negotiations and most interpreted his statements as addressed to Republicans: preparing them for the possibility that the IRA would have to be wound up if Sinn Féin were sufficiently happy with the outcome of the talks.

The response from the DUP was divided: Ian Paisley, Jnr., was negative, but other voices were more positive. Jeffrey Donaldson, the former UUP member who had joined the DUP, appeared on a platform with Martin McGuinness in Donegal, and both said they were looking for a positive outcome to the talks.

The assumption has been made at different stages in this book that these talks will eventually be successful and that devolution will be restored with the agreement of both the DUP and Sinn Féin.

Some conclude from this that the conflict is over. At one level they are correct. Once Sinn Féin takes its place on the Policing Board, then in principle, the conflict *is* over, because this would mean that virtually the entire nationalist community would have accepted the legitimacy of the Police. Further, by taking part in Government Sinn Féin also accepts the legitimacy of the State and the rejection of violence as a means to achieve political ends. However, this does not alter the long-term nationalist ambitions for a United Ireland.

This will mean that the *political* process has succeeded. That is no mean feat. To move from Bloody Sunday and car bombs in the middle of Belfast in the 1970s, the Hunger Strikes in 1980-81, La Mon and Enniskillen (IRA atrocities), Loughinisland and Greysteel (loyalist atrocities), the terrible experience of the Birmingham Six and other people known to have been innocent who were locked up in British jails for many years, to a situation where the idea of the DUP and Sinn Féin being in government together seems almost unsurprising, is an incredible achievement. But success in the political process will not wave a magic wand over the wider divisions in Northern Ireland. As we have seen, segregation widened after 1998. Many believed sectarianism deepened. When the Assembly was in place people in the Community Sector commented on the gap they saw between its work and their needs. They forgot that this is normal in politics. A new devolved government might help reduce sectarianism, but only if the DUP and Sinn Féin act as partners in government instead of trying to run independent fiefdoms, all the time snapping at each other's heels. That can only happen if there is less focus on blaming people for the past, sensitive handling of memorials, an effort to give and take in the funding of different areas, and a willingness to tolerate each other's symbols.

Even with a positive approach from a devolved government people will remain segregated, hurt and suspicious. The fall-out from 35 years of bitter conflict will not disappear overnight, nor for decades. It is vital that this is addressed. We know only too well from the history of the 20th century the human capacity for conflict. Given the history of the Troubles Northern Ireland has three choices:

- To continue as two highly segregated blocs each suspicious of the other.
- To build a civic society which puts enormous emphasis on tolerance, respect and understanding.
- To return to the bitterness of the past.

Of all people we in Northern Ireland should now know the need for a culture of respect, and the difficulties involved both in developing and preserving this.

In the light of this it looks as if there will still be work for Community Dialogue and similar groups. The task now, however, instead of limiting conflict, needs to be more ambitious: to focus on creating a new body politic in Northern Ireland, where there is equality, respect for diversity, and a commitment to protect and cherish all the different groups in the land. That task needs still to be focussed on Unionists and Nationalists. But it also needs to include

Travellers and ethnic minorities, the disabled, and other marginalised groups.

It may be that in time we will be able to lift our heads from the morass of our own local conflict, start respecting and celebrating the diversity we share and perhaps make a contribution to peace in other conflict situations.

Getting Involved in Community Dialogue

Community Dialogue was set up in 1997 - before the Agreement - by people from across the political divide to encourage dialogue about contentious issues arising from the Agreement.

As well as running residentials and seminars we produce leaflets and pamphlets which summarise different views especially of people in the Community Sector .

The aim of our dialogue is not agreement but rather to understand the experience, values, fears and hopes of others.

Our web site contains all our documents: www.communitydialogue.org

If you would like to contact us to take part in dialogues, or to learn more about our work, write, email or phone us at:

Community Dialogue
373 Springfield Road
Belfast BT12 7DG
Tel: + 44 28 28 9032 9995
Fax: + 44 28 9033 0482
Email: admin@communitydialogue.org